Praise for
Un*common H.O.P.E.*

"Dr. Kathleen Hall shares her journey, which in turn sheds light on the journey of divine evolution we are all on, going from who we are to who we can be in a single lifetime. *H.O.P.E.* is the first step on the path that is calling you to your highest self, and you could not have a better guide than one of the most formidable voices for human potential on planet Earth. Don't just read it—live it."

—John St. Augustine, award-winning talk radio host, bestselling author of *Living an Uncommon Life* and *Every Moment Matters*

"Un*common H.O.P.E.* succeeds on every level. Practical, inspirational, informative, and very user-friendly. If ever there was a handbook for getting your life together in these trying times, this is it!"

—Suzanne de Passe, CEO, de Passe Entertainment Group, LLC, Hollywood, CA

"Un*common H.O.P.E.* redefines the activities of a well-lived life. Dr. Hall uses the power of stories and her years of study of the wisdom of others to help us find hope energy—through honesty, optimism, and perseverance—which leads us to joy."

—The Rev. Allen L. Bates, Episcopal priest, Rogers, AR

"Dr. Hall takes you on a very personal spiritual journey that becomes your own. Un*common H.O.P.E.* provides the tools to help cope with our dizzyingly fast-paced world. It's a road map for discovering your authentic self. The journey of a thousand miles begins with THIS step."

—Laurie Cantillo, program director, WABC, New York

"There's no shortage of spiritual guidance out there. But Kathleen isn't about just giving information; she's about living it. And her unwavering passion, energy, and hope are uncommon indeed."

—Terri Trespicio, senior editor, *Body+Soul* magazine

*Un*common
H.O.P.E.

A POWERFUL GUIDE TO CREATING
AN EXTRAORDINARY LIFE

DR. KATHLEEN HALL

Sourcebooks and the colophon are registered trademarks of Sourcebooks, Inc.

Published by Sourcebooks, Inc.
P.O. Box 4410, Naperville, Illinois 60567-4410
(630) 961-3900
Fax: (630) 961-2168
www.sourcebooks.com

Library of Congress Cataloging-in-Publication Data

Hall, Kathleen
  Uncommon H.O.P.E. : a powerful guide to creating an extraordinary life / Kathleen Hall.
     p. cm.
  1. Self-realization. 2. Hope. 3. Happiness. 4. Conduct of life. I. Title.
  BF637.S4H3353 2009
  170'.44—dc22

2009039308

Printed and bound in the United States of America.
BG 10 9 8 7 6 5 4 3 2 1

To my beloved husband,
Jim,
and our daughters,
Brittany Anne
and
Mary Elizabeth,
and my soul mate,
Chloe

Contents

Acknowledgments

So many gifts from others made this book possible.

Thank you Dominique Raccah and Peter Lynch at Sourcebooks for your inspiration and guidance. You challenged me to journey deeper and further, and for that I shall always be grateful.

Thank you also to Judy Kirkwood for your grace and guidance in your editing.

I love you, dear friends, and am grateful for your encouragement and love: Pamela Hayling Hoffman, John St. Augustine, John Ratey, Joyce Newman, and Gina Niederhauser.

I am indebted to my patients and clients who have shared their joys, suffering, gifts, losses, life, and death. You have been my teachers, friends, sheroes, and heroes.

My dear media friends, you have challenged me and gifted me with a public forum, and for that I am humbled and grateful.

I love you and thank you for always being there for me on this life adventure, my dear sisters and brothers, Jon Mark, Jeffrey Dale, Theresa McNamara, and Susan.

I am grateful for the animals at Oak Haven who have been my

four-legged angels that have guided me through many dark nights of the soul. You continue to teach me about love, play, and rest.

Chloe, my partner and soul mate of fifteen years, my devoted Jack Russell, you will always live in my soul.

Thank you to this mystical land of Oak Haven, where angels, saints, and mystics flourish and gift all who visit this ancient Cherokee land.

I am most grateful to my two daughters, Brittany and Elizabeth. Brittany, you have been my Buddha baby since conception. Your Divine gifts of love, tenderness, and healing have crafted you into an amazing physician, who continues to heal and love the sick. Elizabeth, my love for you is unwavering, tested, and true, angel. You have taught me that there really is freedom from suffering.

To Sister Mary and Sister Eleanor at Sacred Heart Monastery, thank you for loving me and teaching me the monastic gifts of love and healing.

Jim, my darling partner and the love of my life, we continue our great adventure together, and it gets more thrilling with each day. Each moment of our lives you make me a better person with your wisdom, love, and radical acceptance. I am humbled to be your life partner. You are a magnificent physician, who is a natural healer to our world.

Thank you, Holy One, for this act of cocreation. It is a sacred privilege experiencing life being present in the Presence in this ancient land.

Mindful Living at Oak Haven

I met Kathleen Hall at a think tank conference of world thought leaders that included Nobel Peace Prize winners, Pulitzer winners, CEOs, astronauts, medical pioneers, and other luminaries. She heard me talk about exercise as a "stress inoculation," and I was riveted by her talk on happiness. *This is different,* I thought. *She's talking about truth and health and committing to being involved in creating a brand-new world.*

She talked about how empty her life was as her career in finance soared, and what happened after she left that world to follow her own path, which took her to Emory University for a master of divinity degree and then on a world tour of monastic, mind-body medicine and meditation and spiritual centers. That eventually led her to establish The Stress Institute and The Mindful Living Network.

Synchronicity is the word I would use to describe our meeting and our work. We continue watering the seeds of our initial conversation as we talk about our discoveries and goals. Kathleen is both a conduit of ancient wisdom for perilous times and a spark for lighting the way home.

After reading Kathleen's book *A Life in Balance: Nourishing the*

Four Roots of True Happiness, I started telling people about the value of "S.E.L.F.," her acronym for self-care: Serenity, Exercise, Love, and Food.

My research in the science of exercise affirms its value not only for a healthy body but also for a healthy mind. As I write in my book *Spark: The Revolutionary New Science of Exercise and the Brain*, "The great thing about exercise is it leaves your body and your mind stronger and more resilient, better able to handle future challenges, to think on your feet and adapt more easily." Human bodies were made for movement, and if we don't get enough of it, we suffer both mentally and physically.

I have focused my work on the value of exercise, but the idea of "serenity" and ways of creating calmness in one's day was new for me personally, and it's huge in mind-body balance. I was familiar with stress-management practices, but was not as serious about practicing things like affirmations, gratitude, and other calming techniques.

To be around Kathleen is to experience love because of her attitude of acceptance. At Oak Haven, the horse farm and home of The Stress Institute and The Mindful Living Network that she created, she fosters animals that have been abused. There may be fourteen dogs and several cats running around her household. The environment remains serene despite the high energy of the dogs (many of which are Jack Russell terriers) and their tendency to do what dogs do, because Kathleen accepts that cleaning up messes is part of life. Much of her wisdom has come from working with the world's rejects, as well as the sick and poor, whether four-legged or two-legged.

The food Kathleen and her husband, Jim, prepare at Oak Haven is simple and nourishing. But what makes it special is the ritual involved in serving and eating each meal. They always sit down to meals. There is always a prayer by Kathleen thanking those who planted, harvested, and cooked the food and expressing gratitude for other gifts of the day, such as a guest's presence. Food is more about the ritual of community and celebration than about merely consuming the food. Preparing the food and washing the dishes is preferably a group activity expressing the joy of cocreating and interdependence.

Kathleen's insights helped me think about some of my own research on our hunter-gatherer ancestors in a new light. We are programmed not only to walk ten to fourteen miles a day but also to gather around the fire or return to the hearth for storytelling and caring about one another. To be interdependent is in our genetic code. And this is what happens at Oak Haven with Kathleen—work, move, eat together, play with the dogs, gather around the fire, and talk. It is primal communion.

In Un*common H.O.P.E.: A Powerful Guide to Creating an Extraordinary Life*, Kathleen continues to illustrate how we can live lives of greater purpose by setting our intentions to be honest, to optimistically accept obstacles as opportunities, to persevere in the midst of our challenges as well as in our callings for work, and to enjoy all of our senses as we go about the daily activities that make up a well-lived life. Her return to ancient wisdom is essential for our survival.

Our first instinct upon meeting each other was to celebrate being human together. When people engage each other, sharing their histories of pain and grief, optimism and joy—the full range of our experiences—sparks fly all over the world. Kathleen is the midwife to a movement—Mindful Living—that is grounded in H.O.P.E. Some ideas have legs. This one, like S.E.L.F., has roots.

John J. Ratey, MD, associate clinical professor of psychiatry at Harvard Medical School, is author of several best selling books on the brain, including *Spark: The Revolutionary New Science of Exercise and the Brain*, and coauthor of *Driven to Distraction: Recognizing and Coping with Attention Deficit Disorder from Childhood to Adulthood*.

The Introduction

The word *hope* conjures up various images in my life's experience. Hope has been an anchor in the midst of the violent, turbulent seas in my ever-changing life. Hope has been a bright, lifesaving lighthouse beacon in the many times I have lost my way in the darkness of my own losses and challenges. Hope is the altar of my life on which I have entrusted my most sacred intentions and adventures. Hope matters.

Hope is real, palpable energy. Each day we experience natural laws of physics that we don't actually recognize, such as wind, light, gravity, and hope. Hope is a natural law of physics and spirituality.

A study examined the relationships between positive emotions and health. Two positive emotions were considered, hope and curiosity, in conjunction with three physician-diagnosed disease outcomes: hypertension, diabetes mellitus, and respiratory tract infections. Across those three disease outcomes, higher levels of hope were associated with a decreased likelihood of having or developing a disease. Higher levels of curiosity were also associated with decreased likelihood of hypertension and diabetes mellitus. These results suggest that positive emotions may play a protective role in the development of disease. As the large body of scientific research continues to grow on mind-body medicine, we will continue to prove the health benefits of this miracle energy called hope.

Hope is the antidote for our confusing world. Hope is evidence of the Divine. Hope is freedom. You can't be in bondage to fear, anger, shame, or uncertainty if you live hope. Anything is possible if you have hope.

I learned about the power of hope from many wells of knowledge and experience.

- *My Ancestors.* My Hall family is a long line of entrepreneurs who were born with the uncanny ability to flourish in any situation. Poverty, world wars, epidemics, illnesses, and death were obstacles that created opportunities for my Hall family. My mother's family, the Clennans, were a culturally rich Irish Catholic family who struggled to make a life on the plains of Kansas against all odds. The constant challenges of brutal prairie life emboldened their strong sense of faith, spirituality, virtue, and love for one another and their community. My DNA is rooted in the precious balm of hope.

- *Nature.* My childhood was rooted in the farmland of Ohio. The cattle that survived the frigid winters birthed the signs of hope as they calved in early spring. The birds seeking out every morsel of food in the snowdrifts of winter chattered in spring as they excitedly created nests and tended to their newborns. The first signs of green grass taunting us through the spring snow brought giggles and expectation as seeds of hope for spring were born. My grandmother's cherry tree was a place of hope eternal as we antici- pated the delicious, red, plump cherries each year and spent rich, memorable hours picking and canning these ruby gifts for a later winter feast. Lying on our backs in the deep grass of summer, we enjoyed lazy afternoons cloud gazing. Each cloud was pregnant with the hope of an animal emerging in the formation. Children naturally know hope is one of the essential elements of our DNA.

- *The Church.* Growing up Roman Catholic was like being a fish in the ocean of hope. (I eventually grew away from my Catholic foundations, but will always be grateful for the many gifts of this religion of hope.) The saints embodied a life of hope. The saints were challenged with torture, sometimes humiliation, and even death, but hope radiated from their souls. Christ became the symbol of hope. He was born of a simple carpenter, became the teacher of love and hope, and eventually his body was killed, but his infectious eternal message of hope lives on. The Mother Mary, a pregnant unwed teen in a conservative Jewish culture, lived hope each day and is still a symbol of love and hope in our world. The seven sacraments of the Church become symbols of hope in every stage of a person's life. The early Church knew how difficult human life was, and I believe they created the sacraments as guideposts of hope to help us navigate our lives. During daily mass I received the sacrament of Holy Communion as incarnational hope in a physical form into my body. The liturgical seasons of the Church taught me that life goes on. To each season of life there are necessary losses, and there is also a celebration of hope in each cycle of life. Advent prepared us for the hope of the coming of Christ at Christmas, and Lent prepared us for the hope of Easter.

- *Storytelling.* Sitting at Clinton's grocery store in Marshallville as a little girl, I was captivated by the stories of hope told by farmers, milkmen, cookie salesmen, and drifters. Some man was pulled out of a burning car at the scene of an accident, a woman got to the hospital just in time to have a C-section and save the baby, or a horrible winter storm just missed us and saved the spring crops. Walt Disney gave the world the gift of hope through his many jewels. Cinderella was joyful and loving as she survived awful stepsisters and a cruel stepmother. Daniel Boone continually saved the lives of the innocent while fighting off bad people and redeeming dark circumstances, giving each of us a sense of hope and goodness in our world.

- *People of Hope.* There were the people who were the physical presence of hope. My aunt Pat had five children and was the night nursing supervisor in our local Dunlap hospital. She worked all night long and would get home in the morning to make us breakfast. She told us stories of what had happened at the hospital that night in the emergency room and in the ICU, and they were always adventures of loss and hope. I wanted to grow up and be just like her. I babysat for Mr. Katz. I would confide in him about the problems in our home, and he would always sit me down and fortify me with hope before he took me home. Dr. Bill Mallard was my professor at Emory who was Dr. Hope. Every time I wanted to throw in the towel, he would literally grab me and take me for a cup of hope. We would sit for hours as he told stories of saints, ancients, professors, and students overcoming tremendous odds with the antidote of hope.

One of my favorite humans, who recently died, Dr. Paul Pearsall, was a neuropsychologist. Dr. Pearsall lived through many cancers, his son's cerebral palsy and eventual death, several near-death experiences himself, and more suffering than most of us will ever know. He has authored many amazing books, and one of my favorite quotes of his is "In the absence of certainty, there is always hope."

WATER IS HOPE

Water has always been a symbol of hope for me. Water is used in the sacraments of the Church, such as baptism, or holy water that blesses us as a sign of favor or hope. Water in the form of rain or snow was always exciting and anointed us with hope. Water as rain or snow nourished our crops, restored our wells, and gave me a great sense of peace and hope in my mind, body, and soul. Water here at Oak Haven, our horse farm, is a source of life for us. Our horses, the birds, the deer and other animals, our gardens, and our crops are graced by these sacred waters. We live at the source of many springs and creeks that converge to form our beautiful Lake Sautee. These springs and creeks flow into our lake, then meander to form the Chattahoochee River, which eventually runs into the Gulf of Mexico.

Water, whether it is a spring, a river, a stream, or an ocean, displays a variety of patterns. These patterns may emerge as ripples, eddies, vortexes, or still, reflective pools of water.

In this work, I have used the metaphor of water as a way to understand our life's journey. I use elements of nature to help us realize that we are one with nature and our lives are a reflection of natural phenomena. We are all linked to a deeper reality. The ancient cultures of our world have always used nature to help us understand ourselves. Jesus, Buddha, Gandhi, Mohammad, and other spiritual leaders use nature and agricultural symbols as they teach us the most crucial lessons of life.

I invite you to journey into the natural flow of your own life. Be curious in this adventure, and trust that the powerful current will lead you to an extraordinary life beyond your imagination.

PART ONE

The River

Just as a great river meanders over the earth with its twists and turns, so does the journey of our precious lives.

The laws of nature drive the water. Sometimes it flows serenely, sometimes it rushes with a force that erodes rock, sometimes it swirls and eddies and pulls us under. Our lives, like the holy rivers of the world, surge and cascade in storms and ebb and trickle during drought. We can attempt to control, plan, or orchestrate the directions of our lives, but they, like the water in the rivers, have their own Divine path.

The challenge for us is to trust the journey of the river of our lives. Eventually we all become one in the sacred journey to the ocean. We may have no more than a raft or a stick of wood to hold on to. But we can trust the waters of the powerful river to guide us home.

The flow of rivers is influenced by the amount of water available, the soil it travels through, the geography of mountains or plains, the gravitational fields in the earth, rain, evaporation, seasons, and so much more. The journey of our lives also has twists and turns with many challenges beyond our understanding or control. Every love, marriage, or child; every experience of betrayal, rejection, or grief; every divorce, illness, or loss; and every holiday, wedding, or funeral in our lives shifts us on a path we may not have mapped out but are destined to travel.

We are like the river, always moving, strong, magnificent, nourishing, and life giving. As long as we breathe, we are moving in a direction. Surrender to the flow and discover the gifts the sacred river has for you.

CHAPTER 1

The Invitation of the River

AN INSUFFICIENT LIFE

Nothing could stop the haunting feeling in my soul that something was wrong with the way I was living my life. My life on the outside looked like the stellar successful life most people on the planet dream of, but from the inside every day was like walking barefoot on jagged rocks.

Seemingly, I had it all. I was intelligent, attractive, and educated. My husband was a loving physician, a "Mr. Mom," caring for the children equally, clearly not the norm in our tier of Southern society. Our home was down the road from the governor's mansion in the best of neighborhoods. I had lots of friends. Our two daughters were healthy, beautiful, and brilliant. I was successful in the business world, working with a prestigious Wall Street firm, and changed cars almost as often as I changed fashions, based on what was new and hot.

But in recent years my anxiety had reached horrendous levels. I began to have full-blown panic attacks, drinking more scotch to keep me calm, but knowing I was at the end of this road. I was miserable, sad, anxious, and hollow. There had to be more meaning to life than going through these rote motions.

None of my roles worked anymore. The roles of wife, mother, professional, and social entrepreneur were empty. I moved from massive levels of guilt to consuming self-loathing. "What the hell is wrong with me? Why can't I be like other women and just be grateful for this comfortable life I have been gifted with?" The more I lamented and repeated this dead-end mantra, the more I knew that I could not continue to live this life. It was parched, dead, and meaningless. I was living an insufficient life.

My daily life was besieged with a sense of wondering and wandering. What made it so intolerable and painful was living with and around people who seemed to be satisfied with living on the surface of life. It was as if everyone had received a menu for their lives at birth and they kept ordering what was on that menu—an education, marriage, children, a "good" job, home, money for retirement, a vacation each year, go to church, pay taxes, don't make any trouble—instead of craving something soulful. For me this was a death sentence. I couldn't stomach the choices on the menu anymore. But how could I tell other people how I felt when I had everything they believed made people happy?

Sometimes the pain was so great it would leak out at a dinner party, at lunch, or at work. The results were always the same: dirty looks, snide comments such as "You are so spoiled," "What is wrong with you? Everybody wants what you have," and "Are you crazy?" All of these responses just increased my sense of isolation and feeling like a stranger in a strange land. I was a prisoner of my well-designed life.

My only soul mates were dead people found in books and biographies—Emerson, Thoreau, Gandhi, Merton, Gregory of Nyssa, Hildegard of Bingen, to name a few. I longed for the depth of their quests and their dedication to live extraordinary lives of meaning and pure experience. With each work I read these monumental souls were alive for me, calling me to have the courage to wake up and choose not to live an insufficient life.

Even as a child I would get passionately lost in stories of saints who went to their death for their radical beliefs on love. Joan of Arc was one of my favorites. I felt as if we were best friends and wished she were alive, because I knew she would understand me.

As a child I climbed and hid in trees, viewing the world from a different perspective. I experienced spiritual transcendence in the branches of an oak tree when, from a distance and high above the fray, I could view life unfolding as I anonymously rested in the safe womb of the tree. I wandered into the woods and built shelters with branches where I could retreat and immerse myself in silence. I was a strange little girl who lived in a world of my own, allowing very few humans into my secret world. All animals were natural members of my tribe, but I was suspicious of two-leggeds with their power, authority, and dominance. Yet as an adult, I had established a life in the midst of the same power, authority, and dominance that I distrusted as a child.

How did I get here? I created a life where I was the queen of my empire and had to take responsibility for my creation. No matter how many loving people showed up in my life, like my husband and children, I still felt I was playing a part in a drama that was not my authentic life. The question was how to stop living this insufficient life and move to living an extraordinary life of purpose.

I had developed business plans for companies and organizations, designed plans for homes and plans for our gardens, plans for education, and the list went on. These plans worked for an outside life in our Western world, but the plans didn't work for a meaningful, soulful life.

I made a promise to myself when I was a child living in a troubled, afflictive family that I would stay in any situation as long as it had hope and energy or a life force driving me. But if the life force evaporated, I could not stay in that life. My mother lived that life of misery. I knew it well. I would not live my mother's life of isolation, sadness, and despair.

So I sat down with a piece of paper and planned my escape from this insufficient life that I had created to a new journey into meaning and experience. Saints, presidents, world leaders, Nobel Peace Prize winners, heroes, or great writers—I made a list of people who lived extraordinary lives of hope and curiosity. I wanted to know what propelled their experiential lives, what drove them, how hope manifested in their lives, and what path they took to get to their destination in life.

I studied their lives until I felt as if I had channeled each of them into my soul and we had relationships and conversations. I collected all the literature and biographies I could find on each person I wanted to explore. After copious study, I then planned how I would travel into each person's life to get a deeper vantage point of their lives. I also sought out people who were scholars or associates of these people who lived extraordinary lives that embodied hope. Whether it was St. Francis, Emerson, or Gandhi, I saw, smelled, and heard the voices of these souls and discovered a Divine family in these wondrous folks.

I created a list of people and places to visit that would be my map as I traveled around the globe for many years on this journey. I felt compelled to experience how my intellectual and spiritual mentors lived and what their physical geography told me about them.

It was clear to me that each person's natural environment had a great effect on nourishing their hope, philosophy, and creativity. I wanted to experience the architecture of their homes, the substance of their gardens, the stock of their libraries, and their culture. I felt the only way for me to discover my new path for my future was to explore my mentors' lives of the past.

I was magically drawn to these magnificent souls and committed to following this adventure. I would craft my life to pursue the bread crumbs of genius they had left for me to discover. I knew these powerful great souls of hope, who had lived extraordinary lives, could teach me and others how to live an extraordinary life, too.

THOREAU'S WALDEN POND AND EMERSON'S CONCORD

"I went to the woods because I wished to live deliberately, to front only the essential facts of life, and see if I could not learn what it had to teach, and not, when I came to die, discover that I had not lived."

This single quote by Henry David Thoreau catapulted me out of the financial business and called me into uncharted waters. I had been trying to manage my chaotic, stressed, busy family life and the financial world for many years. One afternoon after work, in a state of utter exhaustion, I saw Thoreau's book sitting on the bookshelf in my New York apartment. I reached up and opened the book to this quote that would transform my life. I sat paralyzed with tears pouring down my face as I read this quote. If I died today, my insufficient life was running from one fear to another, one success to another, and one drama to another. Thoreau was challenging me to go to the woods and see what I was made of. I heard him say from the grave, "Take your miserable, controlling queen self, and head to the woods, where you will learn what you are really made of."

I wanted to see that ten-foot-by-ten-foot cabin in those Massachusetts woods where Thoreau learned how to live deliberately.

Did I have the courage to shed the trappings of my well-designed life and go to the woods as he did over 150 years ago? A few weeks after reading Thoreau's dramatic charge, I peered into the window of the replica of Thoreau's cabin at Walden Pond. Standing by the glassy, still water, I had one of the most magnificent spiritual experiences of my life. A voice whispered from the mist over the pond, "Go create a place where people come to live deliberately, to learn self-reliance and reverent respect for nature."

In that moment I promised to spend every resource I had—mentally, spiritually, physically, and financially—to create a sanctuary, a Walden Pond, where we curious and confused souls could come to learn ancient truths crucial for a sustainable life of mental, physical, and spiritual health and happiness.

Ralph Waldo Emerson also lived with me daily. His essays and other works became my bible. My pilgrimage to this mentor was another milestone in my quest for meaning. I walked gingerly up to Emerson's home in Concord, Massachusetts, feeling as if I were in an altered world. I sensed the presence of the many great souls that over a century before had traveled from around the world to visit this enlightened guru at his home and gardens. There was a humble sense of gentle genius and sacred solitude. In his time Emerson was extolling words of hope into a world confused by myriad challenges. The rooms and tables where he penned his magnificent words of "Self-Reliance" reminded me of his words:

"God will not have his work made manifest by cowards."

"Trust thyself, every heart vibrates to that iron string."

"Who so would be a man must be a nonconformist."

"Nothing is at last sacred but the integrity of your own mind."

I was home. I had a sense of belonging that I had never experienced. These great souls had committed their lives to create a viable physical place supported with a sustainable philosophy of how to live an extraordinary, authentic life. They bravely experimented with new ideas that would reform society and the world. I was challenged to follow their lead.

JEFFERSON'S MONTICELLO

"I think this is the most extraordinary collection of talent, of human knowledge, that has ever been gathered together at the White House—with the possible exception of when Thomas Jefferson dined alone."

John Fitzgerald Kennedy said this about Thomas Jefferson at a dinner honoring American Nobel Prize winners on April 29, 1962.

Thomas Jefferson was a fiercely free thinker and lived with insatiable hope and curiosity about everything in life. I wanted to see how his experiential nature unfolded at his home in Virginia. Since I couldn't meet him, I felt if I experienced his life through his home, Monticello, I could better understand his genius in the areas of landscaping and gardening, physics, astronomy, writing, inventing, politics, literature, and philosophy.

His love of nature was obvious on the grounds of Monticello. He had kept copious records of the moment each plant bloomed at

Monticello and his intimate experience with each plant. He didn't just observe every plant in his gardens; he tenderly loved and respected each species.

Jefferson's inventions filled each room of his home. His natural propensity to want to know everything about every facet of the universe drew me as I fell in love with his soul. He met no stranger on his life's journey. If a star caught his interest, he lived in astronomy; if a philosophy interested him, he would begin voraciously writing. His mind and soul worked in such a way that he gave incarnational birth to every idea. When he thought about how to change something, he stopped everything and invented something new. He knew no limits. Jefferson lived in the flow of Divine intelligent energy unfolding. He was the midwife to genius.

It was as if he were whispering to me in every room, in every garden, and especially in the cemetery: "Go and create your own Monticello. Be curious, be intentional, and be confident in your journey in this life." I left Monticello beginning to design my own petri dish for studying how to live an extraordinary life.

THE HOLY LAND

My travels took me to Israel, where so many great souls made eternal impressions on humankind. For thousands of years this ancient land has been the source of hope for sacred texts, saints, and leaders. I wanted to experience this land that tribes and cultures have considered so sacred it has been the source of wars and discord since the beginning of history. I wanted to see why this land was so meaningful and crucial to so many throughout history.

I sat on the ground near the rock in Gethsemane, where Jesus prayed before his death and asked God to save his life: "Take this cup from me." He finally surrendered and said, "Let not my will, but your will be done." The raw physical surroundings of ancient olive trees and rugged rocks transported me back in time. I had a primordial sadness and sense of Jesus's painful and humble surrender to his fate, karma, or destiny. I asked myself if I had that kind of courage where I could begin to learn Divine surrender at every turn on this journey. I asked for courage, commitment, and guidance as I rested in this holy place.

I submerged myself in the River Jordan and asked God to wash away my past life and give me the direction for this new path. John and Jesus found these mystical waters life changing. Could they boost my commitment to my quest? The water was freezing, and as I sat on the shore, I did feel a little resurrected. I wasn't birthed, but I knew I was gestating.

I have read the Sermon on the Mount almost every day of my adult life. I believe if everyone on earth read these three simple chapters, Matthew 5, 6, and 7, and lived them daily, all of our lives would be infused with hope, peace, happiness, and love. These chapters hold the wisdom for the world that is reflected in all major world religions and in their leaders.

"You are the salt of the earth; but if salt has lost its taste, how shall its saltiness be restored? It is no longer good for anything, but is thrown out and trampled under foot."

"You are the light of the world. A city set on a hill cannot be hid. No one after lighting a lamp puts it under a bushel, but on the lamp stand, and it gives light to all in the house. In the same way, let your light shine before others, so that they may see your good works and give glory to God in heaven."

Every day of my life I tell myself this: "I am the salt of the earth; live honestly, and be the salt for many. I am the light and keep myself on a stand, not hidden with stuff or issues, so that all can see honest, good work."

I still get goose bumps remembering sitting on the hill by the sea where Jesus said these words that continually inspire and challenge all of us today to live an authentic life.

I had always seen Jesus as a kind of radical homeless hero of the disenfranchised who lived on the margins of society planting the seeds of hope into souls of the past, present, and future. Jesus lived an extraordinary life of truth and challenged the comfortable societies throughout history to wake up, take responsibility for their lives, and learn how to love one another and hope for a better world. Whatever I was to build, the place must be in the majestic power of nature, and the teachings must teach people to live honestly and "be the salt," and to continually "be the light" in this wounded world.

ST. FRANCIS OF ASSISI

St. Francis is one of my all-time favorite saints, so I had a strong desire to visit Assisi, Italy. I had taught about St. Francis at Emory and through his work and the literature felt his presence quite frequently guiding me. He was one of the great souls I wanted to emulate in building a new center in nature that incorporated his concepts of creation and love.

His beliefs about everything in nature being part of God were radical. St. Francis proclaimed:

"We are sister and brother to animals and plants, water and soil, earth and sky."

I wanted to create a place that reflected St. Francis's philosophy. In my model people could immerse themselves in nature and experience it as their loving, trusted family instead of a place foreign to themselves. The idea would be to offer a space where the natural world and humans were on equal footing in a community that reflected the notion that we are one seamless thread of creation.

This story of St. Francis has always melted my heart. St. Francis grew up as the son of a wealthy cloth merchant in Assisi. After Francis's release from prison during one of the many local wars, he began regularly singing, praying, and walking alone. Many in Assisi believed young Francis had gone mad. He began to have visions and heard the voice of God saying, "Rebuild my church." Francis's father, outraged at this embarrassing behavior, called him to the town square to humiliate Francis in front of the entire town. After surviving the shame and fury of his father in front of all of Assisi, Francis said, "You are no longer my father. God is my father. I give you back my name, all of my earthly belongings, even the clothes on my back." He removed all of his clothing and stood naked in the square. Francis left the square naked and barefoot, walking into the snow to become one of the most beloved saints in history.

My entire body and soul were vibrating the minute I arrived in Assisi. I didn't sleep for the first three days I was there, experiencing the "thin space" I had read about. The Celts described thin space as the holy spaces on our planet where the Divine is totally present and can be experienced. A prized, rare thin space is a sacred portal between heaven and earth. The birds sang and flew around all night long on my porch. I felt sure it was a sign from St. Francis to me saying, "Yes."

One evening I couldn't read the Italian menu as we tried to order our dinner at an adorable café on the edge of the mountain. I was frustrated trying to translate each item when a soft voice from behind me whispered, "Can I help you with that?" I turned around to see a thin, middle-aged man eating alone at a tiny table next to the open window. "I have come here for years and know the language pretty well. I can read the menu for you if you like." As he began to read the menu, I asked him to join us so we could find out more about him and Assisi.

Father Tim was from the United States. He had been taking sabbaticals to Assisi for most of his priesthood. We had a wonderful dinner talking about St. Francis, theology, Italy, and the state of the world. In conversation I asked him, "How long will you be here this time?" He answered, "I am close to my death, and I will die here in Assisi. I have a terminal disease and am at the very end now. I decided there couldn't be a place closer to heaven than Assisi and chose to be here as I move on to the other side."

After a piercing silence, he asked if I wanted to walk the old cobblestone streets of Assisi with him as the sun set. We walked for hours, laughing, crying, and sharing gifts from our journeys. As I hugged Father Tim's frail body to say good-bye, I could sense he would die very soon. I stayed up all night long on our porch as the birds flew past my face in the night. I knew I had met a saint. For the life of me I couldn't figure out if he was real or a "being" sent to guide me further on the journey.

St. Francis's form of monasticism drove his monks into hermitages in the mountains, where they practiced an action-reflection method. They would pray, contemplate, and renew at the hermitages but then travel the countryside preaching and teaching words of love, compassion, and hope. St. Francis's theological underpinnings were tethered to nature and the natural world. He believed that we experience the

Divine in nature and that it has a transformative power. I knew I wanted to recapitulate his work in my life some way and somewhere in my future. I wanted to create a modern-day hermitage where people could come to experience St. Francis's invaluable gifts to us.

NATIVE AMERICAN JOURNEYS

Gloria was my Native American friend who guided me on my path into the theology of the Native people. She lived in the Sautee Valley, in the North Georgia Mountains, the home of the ancient Cherokee, with her fourteen children. Gloria's waist-length, raven hair was tediously braided to perfection. She was one of the most beautiful women I have ever met, both inside and outside.

I met Gloria when I visited her store that sells authentic Native American jewelry, artifacts, pottery, sculpture, and clothing. Two pairs of earrings interested me: one was turtles, and the other bears. It was obvious that I couldn't make up my mind. She leaned across the counter and asked, "Well, do you need turtle energy or bear energy in your life?"

"Turtle energy is grounded in Mother Earth, flexible, able to live in water and on earth," Gloria said. "Bear energy calls you to introspection, going to the cave. Do you need to go within?"

I pushed both pairs toward her and pulled out my wallet. "I'll take both please."

That was the beginning of a long, rich friendship, and she became one of the greatest mentors of my life. Gloria taught me about animal totems and Native American theology and how she incorporated that into her Catholicism. She became my primary source of wisdom and guidance on this journey into the land of the soul.

Gloria inspired me to travel around the country and experience various Native American cultures. Travels to the Four

Corners—Arizona, New Mexico, Utah, Colorado—and Alaska transformed my life in magnificent ways. I stayed with many different tribes and learned a sacred way of experiencing nature.

The Divine is in every cell of nature. Animals are sacred symbols, signs, and lessons from the Divine. When a hawk flies overhead, be silent and listen; the sacred hawk is delivering a message from the Divine to you. When a rabbit runs in front of your car, the rabbit reminds us to look fear in the face. The Hopi, Navajo, Ute, Zuni, Cherokee, Creek, Shawnee, Ojibwa, Aleut, and Tlingit share ancient rituals of sweat lodges, vision quests, and fire. Native people teach us reverent respect for everything in creation; everything has meaning, from a piece of quartz to a feather to sage. In a nanotechnology world, Native cultures open the door to mindful living and give us hope for the future of our wounded world.

At every turn in my travels I kept a notebook and wrote down what fascinated me. There was a central theme with each teacher and his or her philosophy. Each person I studied was committed to living an extraordinary life. Their lives were rooted in awareness, reverent respect for all life, and hope for the future. I wanted to create a center where I could integrate the best teachings of these great souls so people could come to learn how to live an extraordinary life.

It was essential to begin my journey at a basic core level in nature. I was committed to taking the long road, because I didn't want to miss anything along the way. I wanted to directly confront my fear, anger, shame, and control issues. If I was going to be able to teach these incredible truths, I would have to begin at the beginning, in the rawness of nature, in uncharted territory and pure experience.

There was no looking back. I left my carefully orchestrated life.

The time for research and travel was over, and it was time to challenge my fears and begin the action of creating my new life. I purchased a small primitive cabin with no water, no plumbing, and no power on 250 acres of woods in the North Georgia Mountains.

"The journey of a thousand miles begins with one step."

CHAPTER 2

Living in the River

One of the things I learned from studying extraordinary people was that they don't hide from their fears, but face them. So I decided to write down the things I feared most in life and confront them straight on. My list of fears included being alone, being poor, having no status, letting go of control, being in the woods, and going outside during the night.

I knew what I had to do. I would stay at a log cabin for three to four days a week by myself so I could face my demons. It was the only way. I had to face the fears that were controlling my life: bare, raw, and directly. My greatest fear was being alone.

But there was one massive hiccup in my desire to create this new life. I had the responsibility of two young daughters and a supportive husband. We had a family meeting. Your family knows when you are not happy, and it was abundantly clear that I was miserable and had to do something different. I posed our family dilemma this way. "If we continue the way we are living now, you can have about 5 percent of me for as long as this lasts, which may not be long. But if we choose to go on this family adventure, you will probably have 100 percent of me for the rest of our lives." We would be together as much as possible, but at this time, I had to face my demons and follow this journey.

We carefully planned our family journey and addressed the challenges it would present. We hired a wonderful housekeeper, Ernestine. We had a family calendar with all of our important family events such as sporting events, church functions, holidays, ice cream rituals, and special time together.

The girls loved Ernestine, and she was magical as part of our family. They were busy at school during the day, and it was easy to slip into town at night when they needed me. Jim had always been a "Mr. Mom," so his role didn't change. The girls loved coming to the farm each weekend to see what we had built and discover the new animals we had rescued or found. We were all very close, and the key was our focus on communication. When one of us had a problem or challenge, we talked about it a lot and sought family counseling when we needed it.

A great odyssey was unfolding as I entered this strange land in the woods.

My friends warned me my physician husband would run off with a nurse if I did this, or he would flat-out divorce me. Others said my children would fail in school and turn into drug addicts or serial killers if I didn't play the role of devoted wife and mother. I had my moments of guilt, grief, terror, anger, and despair—lots of them.

So I sought out readings about women who had created different lives, as I was doing. Anthropologist Jane Goodall lived with chimpanzees for years. Social activist Dorothy Day slept in bug-infested shelters with workers in New York. Most of the mystics and saints lived very unconventional lives. Rachel Carson lived in the wild. And Louise Hay created a haven for the sick and afflicted and went on to become a great healer and leader. I identified with these mavericks who had lived nontraditional, extraordinary lives.

I shed all the trappings of society and the graceful life of privilege I had orchestrated for many years. The first night I spent in the cabin alone in the wilderness was terrifying. There were no lights, no running water. I had a candle and bottles of water, and there was only an outhouse for the bathroom. I chastised myself for putting myself in this horrifying experience. But I really knew within the depths of my soul that this experience would change me forever. I had to go deep within myself to discover what I was made of and who I was. I wanted an authentic life, and this was the real deal. I did not sleep at all the first night. I spent the night sitting in a chair trying to control my panic attacks and slow down my crazed mind. It was interesting to observe my terror and panic. Every moment in that paralyzing darkness was torture as I prayed for the first ray of daylight.

The real horror was when I heard animals walking on the dry leaves outside the window in the pitch dark. My mind rushed, creating murderers, hunters ready to shoot me, or some rare killer animal ready to eat me. All of this was quite different from the beautiful home with the intricate alarm system in Buckhead, Atlanta, I was used to.

When the early morning sunlight filtered into the cabin window, I felt safe and surrendered into a deep sleep. I woke up in the late morning to the sound of something walking on leaves outside my window. As I hesitantly peeked out the window, there stood a doe with her fawn. I melted with overwhelming tenderness. I felt as if I had climbed a great mountain and was a champion. The doe and her fawn were a sign from heaven that everything was going to be all right.

I opened the cabin door, took a deep breath of sweet mountain air, and headed to WalMart and purchased four pairs of blue jeans, boots, shirts, and warm socks. I went to the local general store and asked where I could find a handyman to help me. The owner told me there was a great old man who lived on the farm next to us. I got his phone number and called him. He was excited about helping me, and I felt like I had crossed another huge hurdle.

I hired JC, the wonderful old man who lived next door, to teach me how to work the land. This simple farmer was a wise sage on my journey.

Thin, crusty, tough, and angelic, JC taught me to look at bugs, worms, trees, and animals to determine the weather forecast. He taught me how to live in this new wildness. He was my teacher as we put in plumbing, electricity, and heat; harvested our spring for water; and chinked the old cabin. My hands told the story of my new life: scratches, no fingernails, splinters, blisters, and parched skin. Hard physical labor I had never known was the design of each day.

JC never complained when I'd call him in the middle of the night in my panicked states. Sometimes it was a bear banging on the side of the cabin door or a coyote howling outside on the hill by the cabin or a snake coiled on the porch telling me to go home.

He always came when I called. Always. He was faithful, true, and my rock.

Jim and the girls came up to the farm every Thursday or Friday and we spent the weekends together. On Mondays when they left we would look at our calendar to see if I would be down to Atlanta for a game, dinner, or family event. Our family had a fluid life back and forth between the farm and Atlanta. Each of us began to notice the different life we were creating. We all worked on the land, rode horses, watched the sunset, made lots of homemade ice cream, and laughed a lot at our struggles and our continual surrender to the elements and power of nature.

Weeks turned into months, and after a year I knew I was onto something big. My life was completely different. Previous evenings of anxiety and emptiness were now replaced with a rocking chair on the back porch watching pastel sunsets over the mountains. My chronic insomnia diminished as the crickets and loud bullfrogs lulled me to sleep every night.

When I panicked—and believe me, I was the queen of panic attacks—I would hold a dog or cat and take deep, long breaths until it eventually subsided. My panic attacks had become rare, and the intensity was so much less.

I noticed the powerful new rhythm of my life was transforming my soul, my marriage, and our family. When I first arrived at the cabin, my mind would race as I experienced my emotions flowing into chaos. Next, the uncontrollable state of hellish panic hit. But these days, instead of reacting, I was slowly learning to surrender and not react to the panic. *Surrender* was a bad word for me in my past life based on success and status. It meant to lose. I was learning that surrender is a powerful spiritual experience, and each time I surrendered I entered a sea of grace, peace, and hope. Surrender became one of the most powerful tools in my tool shed, along with its twin, meditation.

I learned that surrender is the first step toward freedom and renewed strength. When we surrender we open ourselves up to the Divine plan, which is bigger and more mysterious than anything we could ever conjure up. The more you practice surrender, the stronger you become.

I also learned to surrender to the animals. They were teaching me the natural rhythm of life. My fear of the animals that lived here in the woods had transformed into curiosity, tenderness, reverent respect, and love. When I heard a scratchy noise at night, I would open the door or window and curiously investigate my nocturnal visitor.

I had finally befriended this wild natural world. She was my teacher, I was her student, and she had much to teach me. I imagined her as one of my beloved professors. And as I grew, every living thing in creation was my family.

I had stepped into the river. There was no fighting the current.

CHAPTER 3

Navigating the River

My consistent anxiety was hard to manage. I was exercising, praying, and staying in nature, but my mind continued to race. Reading works by the mystics and monastics like Teresa of Avila, Thomas Merton, and Thomas Keating gave me hope that centering prayer and meditation would be some help for this horrible plague of anxiety.

A friend of mine told me about a Taoist monk in Atlanta who was teaching meditation and healing. She told me this monk was a kind and gentle teacher. She promised to go with me for my first session.

My heart was racing as we walked into the back of the room of the home where the class was held. A young girl handed me a cushion. This was new territory for me, and I wanted to make sure no one noticed me as I slithered as far against the back wall as anyone could go. We sat in stark silence as my heart raced to over one hundred beats a minute. I kept telling myself this was ridiculous, but something at the depths of my soul was telling me my life was about to change forever. I had lived my life in institutional religions smattered with academic pursuits in traditional academic institutions. This was all terrifying foreign territory for me.

A small man in a soft beige robe bowed to the group of forty people in the room, and then he gently settled to the floor in the lotus position and went immediately, without words, into silence.

No instruction, no directions. I wondered what in the world was going on. We sat there for at least twenty minutes. When he finally opened his eyes, he broke the silence with the ring of a bell. Looking up he immediately asked, "Who is this new person in the back row with the brown sweater?"

My worst fears were realized. I wanted to hide in the back, undiscovered, invisible, unknown, and now he brought the focus of the entire group to me. I was an outsider, a foreigner, a visitor, hiding in the shadows. Everyone turned and stared. He asked my name, and I sputtered it out quickly with a tremor in my voice. That was followed with two more questions by the teacher: "Why are you here, Kathleen? What do you want to learn?"

With no prepared answer for these questions I answered my new teacher in a measured tone, "I am here to learn meditation. My mind races out of control, and I would love to learn to be peaceful."

He smiled widely and said, "Welcome, Kathleen. You are at the right place."

That was the first day of over seven years of studying with my teacher, Wong Loh Sin See. He became my guide into the world of sacred silence, holy listening, and healing others and myself.

He was a magnificent teacher and said he was preparing me to become a teacher someday. He offered patience and gracious kindness to me. I had never experienced such tenderness and caring in a man or a teacher before. The longer I studied and practiced meditation and healing practices, the more I experienced powerful emotions floating to the surface, crying out to be recognized, blessed, and released.

In the beginning of my journey into meditation my thoughts popped up every second. It was driving me mad. But then after a week there were small, pregnant pauses in my practice. I cried intermittently, experienced anger and frustration frequently, and eventually surrendered to the process of healing.

As the years passed I moved from the beginner class to the intermediate and on to the advanced class. Each session began with twenty to thirty minutes of silence broken by the teacher asking profound questions about our human condition: "Why are we jealous and want what belongs to others?" "What do you fear when you enter into the river of meditation?" Students would give their best answer to a posed question. A teaching from the question would follow. Again we would enter into a twenty- to thirty-minute meditation, with the teacher ending with a blessing on his students.

After years of training, I developed a keen sense of the flow of energy in the body and learned how to sense disease in the body, whether physical (for example, a tumor) or an energy blockage. I learned how energy moves and how to help it travel. Taoism taught me that life is all about energy balance and imbalance. I would spend hours in a single meditation, days in healing trainings, and years in practice, practice, and more practice.

After Taoism, a wonderful nun I met introduced me to Buddhism. A group of nuns invited me to go with them to study with a famous monk named Thich Nhat Hanh. I was smitten with his tenderness and compassion and became a student of Thich Nhat Hanh. I continued my study of Buddhism and meditation and other spiritual practices as his student. This was one of my greatest adventures into self-discovery.

Thich Nhat Hanh is a very loving and compassionate being. I learned that saying angry words, eating meat, thinking unkind thoughts, drinking alcohol, and watching violent movies can create violence in your life and in relationships with those you love. The Buddhists believe that everything a person thinks, eats, drinks, and says affects the cultivation and peace of his soul. I wanted to experiment and see how I would change if I quit eating meat and stopped drinking alcohol. It has been many, many years, and these practices have been transformative.

His Holiness the Dalai Lama visited Emory regularly, and I learned about Tibetan Buddhism. Much of my learning with His Holiness was about the mental, physical, and spiritual effects of meditation. He loves science and research on meditation, so this was integrated into his talks. In recent years I have enjoyed his conferences that have focused on the medical research on the healing effects of meditation in most diseases. It is especially effective in stress and depression conditions.

The Dalai Lama influenced me with his work on compassion. I had always had compassion for other people but never for myself. I learned that the seed of compassion must be planted in your own heart first. You nourish it, fertilize it, water it, and it grows to encompass family, friends, community, and the world. When you center yourself in compassion, the result is a ripple effect.

What could I do with this incredible training, and what were my next steps to creating a center where people could learn to live an extraordinary mindful life every day? I knew I needed some type of formal education besides my bachelor of science degree in finance. Progressive world leaders often taught and lectured at Emory in Atlanta. I needed to learn about spirituality, theologies, and counseling, so enrolling in Emory's master of divinity program seemed like a good place to begin.

I attended Emory and balanced our farm life with living in the city. Our girls were in high school and involved in sports, so we all had a very busy, organized life. Our family loved the farm, and we spent as much time as we could there during my following three years at Emory.

I loved studying theology and spirituality. My favorite class was Early Church History, and eventually the professors asked me to become a teaching assistant. Along with attending classes at Emory I chose to immerse myself in extracurricular community service at various places to experience different types of suffering firsthand. I facilitated a group at the Atlanta Battered Women's Shelter, worked at the Atlanta Women's Day Shelter, and became a chaplain at Northside, St. Joseph, and Scottish Rite's children's hospitals. My daughters accompanied me many of the times I worked at my placements. I felt it was essential for their development to work with other populations who live daily in suffering.

This educational experience was absolute heaven. To my surprise, I was especially drawn to the ancient wisdom of the early monastics. The systems of ancient Rome—religions, governments, and feudalism—were oppressive. Courageous people who lived centuries ago also believed they were living insufficient lives. They chose to leave the urban areas and go into the wilderness to discover a more meaningful way of life. They faced their fears in order to discover an authentic, extraordinary life of love. Hope is the essence of monastic thinking and living. Every step of the way, I felt this was the wisdom that could reform and renew our selves, our families, and our society.

Monastic spirituality made me feel at home, understood, accepted, and loved. The monastics lived a whole life of happiness grounded in the Divine rhythm of nature. Each day was rooted in the rhythm of meaningful rituals. I loved this work so much my professors asked me to become a teaching assistant and teach ancient wisdom under them the next year.

While attending Emory, I began working on plans for developing our farm, which we had named Oak Haven. Our property is covered with ancient oaks and tucked back from the world and is a haven for all animals, plants, and humans. Oak Haven was a perfect name for this new center we were going to create.

CHAPTER 4

Stops on the River

An essential part of my training had to be my experiencing other people's suffering. While I was at Emory my advisor designed a program where I could observe, participate, and learn about the range of human suffering. I had experienced great suffering and abuse in my own childhood. I learned that not only can we survive suffering, but we can also transmute it. Not only can we create abundant lives for ourselves, but we can also learn to help others who suffer. I lived in the womb of my own suffering but became fascinated with how others handle suffering. I wanted to make sure I had not created a life running from suffering. Creating a program where I had to sit with people's tremendous suffering could be healing, I thought.

So I spent years of my life in the bowels of suffering. Little did I know how life-changing, horrible, and dark this experience would turn out to be.

THE BATTERED WOMEN'S SHELTER

As a facilitator at the Atlanta Battered Women's Shelter, I witnessed some of the grisliest cases of abuse and suffering one can imagine.

Victims included a woman whose husband had gotten angry with her and wanted her wedding ring back. She couldn't get her ring off, so he put her hand down a garbage disposal trying to remove the ring. Another woman's husband chained his wife in their attic for a month, feeding her like a dog with tiny bits of food in a dog dish. The horrors men did to the women they professed to love were unimaginable. Week after week I would sit in our support group as my head would spin with horror. As I left each session, I could hardly drive home. My angelic husband would fill up the bathtub with hot water, help me undress, and sit with me as I tried to soak out the horrors I had witnessed from my body and soul.

As painful as this experience was, it played a large role in my healing process, since I came from a violent childhood. I relived the terror of my childhood through the pain of these women. It was hard to separate their pain from mine. I never thought I could survive reliving my past, but I did. I thought I had escaped the torture of my childhood, but these women helped me relive my terror each week. These courageous women helped wash away the horror of my own experience, healed me, and made me strong again.

HOSPITALS

After the Battered Women's Shelter, I worked as a chaplain at a children's hospital, where I worked in the cancer ward with tiny souls betrayed by life. The suffering of their families was heart-wrenching.

I walked into rooms of children struggling to live day after day. I sat on the edge of Julie's bed, her big brown eyes staring at me though she was too weak to talk. I nodded my head at her mother sitting exhausted in the chair as I touched Julie's frail hand. Leukemia had ravaged her thin, four-year-old body. With death imminent it is difficult, if not impossible, to find words to comfort a mother. At this stage each visit was a hug, a smile, tears, or a soft silence.

I would dread my beeper going off, because it meant a child had died or the nurse wanted me there at the end with the family. It was 9:30 Wednesday night when my beeper went off to tell me Julie was gone. I jumped in my car, but by the time I got to her room everyone was gone. The room was empty, bed stripped, and only a small dried plant stood in the corner of the barren room. The smell of death was recognizable. I shrunk into the chair where Julie's mother had sat just a few hours before and wept. I was the mother of two daughters, so it was impossible not to identify with each mother's devastation.

My next assignment was to be a chaplain for the cancer and AIDS floor in another large hospital. Everyone I worked with was in some stage of dying.

Tony was my first terminal AIDS patient. The first day I walked into his room I was terrified. His skin was covered with open sores, and his emaciated body was hard to look at. I vacillated between two conflicting desires: should I avoid looking at his ravaged body or stare at this horrible disease I had never seen?

Tony's eyes were closed, so I tried to sneak out and recoup in the hall. Just as I touched the handle of the door, he whispered softly, "Hi, who are you?" Adrenaline rushed through my body. "I am Kathleen Hall, the chaplain. I'm here to see if you need anything or if there is anything I can do for you."

"I've been alone since I've been here. No visitors. Could you just sit with me for a while?" So I sat. What Tony told me taught me so much about death, AIDS, and fear. His family and partner had rejected him, so he had gone through his entire death experience alone. My heart broke experiencing his sense of rejection, isolation, and abandonment.

I promised Tony I would be his partner for the rest of his tenuous life. For the next week I read to Tony, fed him, laughed with him, sat in silence with him as the television flashed in the background. The nurse beeped me one night and told me Tony was tired. It was near the end, and he wanted me with him. I headed to Tony's side. I sat holding his head in my arms as he took his last breaths on this side of life.

What a privilege it had been to share life with Tony. After he died, I sat on the chair as they took his body away. Again, the only thing left in the room was a plant. There was a small voice that whispered, "Take my plant as a sign that I lived. Please take me with you and remember me."

That was eighteen years ago, and I still water and feed "Tony" as he sits in the corner of our family room. Tony lives in that plant, and I talk to him regularly and thank him for being my teacher.

I had experienced tremendous suffering and loss as a chaplain. Most times I felt like the Angel of Death. I felt despondent, worthless, and powerless to help heal these people. I sat in the midst of the worst moments of many people's lives—the space between life and death. All I could do was listen, hold them, love them, and be a witness to their suffering.

One day I just couldn't take it anymore. I walked into the chaplain's office for some support and advice from a well-respected superior. Reverend Judy Wolfe gave me a plaque that day, and I still have it on my wall behind me. It reads: "I can do no great things, only small things with great love. —Mother Teresa." That has become one of the mantras of my entire life.

ORDINATION

I returned for a graduate degree to learn about spirituality, divinity, religions, and what made the soul world tick. Ordination never crossed my mind. Cindy, a United Methodist minister, kept asking me to consider being ordained. The more we talked about it, the more I realized what an opportunity it would be for me to develop skills that could help people in a profound way. It could also give me more training in pastoral care, where I could experience listening and guiding people through suffering.

By this time I had enough experience and training to know I was called to care for people with mental, physical, and spiritual suffering. It took two years of preparation for ordination—research, supervision, counseling, education, constant evaluations, and training. It was a privilege, a blessing, and a tremendous responsibility to serve others as an ordained minister.

PASTORAL CARE

After ordination, I was in a church of three thousand people for several years. I performed the pastoral care and was responsible for our inner-city work. It was immensely rewarding. I loved teaching, preaching, celebrating sacred rituals, providing pastoral care for the people, and working with the inner-city disadvantaged.

People's suffering and stress levels continued to fascinate me. It was astounding to see how much misery a person was willing to tolerate. The mind-body connection interested me tremendously, so I began studying integrative medicine in my spare time. People's psychological and spiritual problems were affecting their health in horrendous ways. I wanted to learn more about the mind-body connection and the effects of spiritual practices on mental and physical health. I needed more education in this area but was clearly in love with spirituality. It was time for me to leave full-time ministry to pursue more education and training in the emerging field of mind-body medicine, which captivated me.

DOCTOR OF SPIRITUALITY

I pursued a doctorate in spirituality at Columbia Theological Seminary after I left the United Methodist Church. I was intrigued with the connection between people who engaged in spiritual practices and their health outcomes. There was emerging scientific research on the health benefits of such things as meditation, journaling, nature, listening to music, positive affirmations, guided imagery, tai chi, chi gong, yoga, and acupuncture.

Bill Moyers had done the PBS television special *Healing and the Mind*, interviewing mind-body experts about their research. I called each one of the centers featured in one segment of the special called "Wounded Healers": Rachael Remen, MD, at Commonweal; Herb Benson, MD, Harvard Mind/Body Institute; Dean Ornish, MD, the Preventive Medicine Institute; Jon Kabat Zinn, PhD, University of Massachusetts Center for Stress Reduction; and Nicholas Hall, PhD, psychoneuroimmunologist. I spent four years attending clinical trainings at these medical centers integrated with academic exercises on spirituality.

During these years I also decided to investigate alternative medicine practitioners: people who did Reiki, energy healers, aromatherapists, herbalists, kinesiologists, polarity healers, acupuncturists, and massage therapists who practiced various types of massage.

Entering a two-year program to become a certified spiritual director was next. Before I began to build a center for mindful living, I felt I needed to have training in spiritual direction under my belt. I spent two years writing papers on silence, spiritual direction, and spiritual discernment models interspersed with reporting to spiritual directors groups and being under supervision.

It was time to leave the ivory towers of education, training, and experience and begin the challenging task of synthesizing all I had learned and gathered from this very long intentional journey.

When you are curious and love education, training, and new experiences, it is easy to stay in school forever. I had become accustomed to this educational-training lifestyle. It was time for me to get out of my comfort zone of being the perpetual student and studying with the masters. It was time for me to become the teacher.

All of the elements were amassed: enumerable years of education, training, experience, and the perfect place to build the learning center. It was time to fly out of the safety of the nest and create the Hermitage at Oak Haven.

CHAPTER 5

The River Leads Home

Our disoriented world is crying out for ancient wisdom. Spiritual traditions have shown resilience for thousands of years. The ancient monastics, as well as the pillars of Eastern religions and Native American cultures, plus Jefferson, Emerson, Thoreau, and St. Francis, had left a map for how to live an extraordinary life of hope, joy, and freedom. I had been designing a center for mindful living and stress reduction in my head and on paper. It was time to build Oak Haven, the Center for Mindful Living.

THE HERMITAGE

Years were spent gathering education, training, and experience to create Oak Haven. I felt like Lewis and Clark traveling, exploring, and keeping copious records of my adventures for future use. Oak Haven is my contribution to "Where Science Meets the Soul." The Hermitage, the Center for Mindful Living, was constructed according to ancient traditions, so all who visit are entering a place of rich, magnificent, natural balance. Ancient wisdom, modern science, and nature are at the foundation of Oak Haven.

The monastic traditions of Buddhism, Christianity, Hinduism, and Taoism foster a life of stability, sustainability, health, hope, joy, and love. Their commitment to spiritual practices teaches us how to live in the Divine rhythm of life, from which we have been disconnected for a very long time.

We long to connect to the holy rhythm of life and yearn to experience the pulsating cadence of power and meaning within our souls. We cry out for some sense of stability in a chronically volatile world. The spiritual practices of the monastic life create health and happiness. The core of the monastic life is love of self, love of God, and love of community. Each of these is inextricably woven into the tapestry of monasticism.

Oak Haven is the integration of scientific research and profound spiritual practices woven into a spectacular sanctuary in nature in the North Georgia Mountains. Every facet of life here has a purpose and is treated with reverent respect. The daily rhythm includes holy devotion, holy food/feast, holy work (cocreation), holy study, holy leisure, and holy sleep. All of these holy facets of the day lead to a whole, complete life of balance, order, and meaning.

This sacred system of rhythm literally saved my life and the life of my family. The monastic cycles keep me moving through each day, flowing with great awareness and gratitude through every moment of my life.

HOPE AT OAK HAVEN

Oak Haven is the center for hope and H.O.P.E. I arrived here many moons ago with the hope that I could learn how to live a life rich with meaning and love and not be kept hostage from my life's purpose. Since that time my DNA and the DNA of Oak Haven have merged into a river of hope.

Every rescued dog, cat, or horse has found hope. Cancer patients, cardiac patients, inner-city children, business leaders, people from all walks of life have discovered new hope at Oak Haven. It doesn't matter what wounds or challenges you bring to Oak Haven—there is infectious hope that washes away the parasites that are eating away the life you were meant to live.

The acronym H.O.P.E. was birthed at Oak Haven at the Hermitage on the side of the lake. After many years of listening to the pain, suffering, joy, and challenges in people's lives I discovered a simple acronym that distills how to live the extraordinary life you desire: Honesty, Optimism, Perseverance, and En-joy.

Honesty is the basis for a life of love and meaning. The serenity and peace of Oak Haven are rooted in honesty. If you are not honest, you can never experience true peace and love. Each of us has our own truth and can begin to live a life of pure honesty at any moment.

With **O**ptimism, every obstacle is an opportunity. Oak Haven is the essence of the natural world. Nature is filled with obstacles daily, whether a flood, erosion, drought, or loss of animal life. Each time we face an obstacle, an opportunity emerges to forge new relationships with others, learn something new, or bring new life to Oak Haven.

Perseverance is the basis of nature. You can mow the pastures at Oak Haven today, and in just a few weeks you will be doing it again. Nature is a model of perseverance, and it sets the stage for the people who come here from all over the world who must learn how to become resilient.

We live **E**n-Joy (in joy) every moment here at Oak Haven. It is pure joy as the birds eat seed from the bird feeders, the mare nurses her foal, the hawk circles over the lake, or a deer runs across the pasture. We teach people who arrive to discover joy in the simple things in life such as washing the dishes, taking a shower, or driving on their daily commute.

My travels were over. My work was becoming centered at Oak Haven. But this was not the end of a journey. It was the beginning of another river, which bubbled out of the earth to become Oak Haven's Lake Sautee, which fed other new rivers.

PART TWO

The Spring

Hope springs eternal. Hope is like springwater bubbling out of the earth—you cannot stop it. It erupts in the most unlikely scenarios of human tragedy—war, the Holocaust, hurricanes, and tornados. It accompanies conception as our bellies swell and ripen, and flows through families as children change and grow. A powerful and potent spiritual practice, once tapped, hope does not go back underground, but fills up whatever will hold it and keeps flowing.

Springwater from the source is often pure and rich in minerals, which is why Evian in France is a mecca for fans of bottled water. But different springs tell different stories. A spring with no path grows stagnant. Springs have to be tapped, or harvested, in order to be vital and for their power to be harnessed.

Oak Haven happens to have an amazing spring that is an abundant source of water for the property, serving humans, animals, and the landscape. The spring is the beginning of the Sautee Creek that flows through the valley, the original home of the ancient Cherokee Nation. It meanders into the Chattahoochee River, providing water for several states before emptying into the ocean.

It wasn't long before JC, the old farmer next door, came over to teach me how to harvest the spring in order to channel the water. We dug deep down into the spring and put a large tank into the ground to hold this sweet, pure water. The pressure underground keeps the water continually flowing.

What at first looked like a trickle emerging from the earth turned into thousands of gallons of water. If a spring does not flow or is not harvested and piped to another river, stream, or lake, stagnant standing water develops, which poses a danger for livestock, as they can get stuck in the soft, wet mud. I learned that if I didn't address the problem at the source, it would become a trap.

A Native American chief told me that our spring was believed to be sacred with mystical healing properties. I often wonder, as I drink this fresh water, about all the interesting souls through time who have sat beneath this sycamore tree and shared this same life source. I raise a toast to all of us, past, present, and future. And especially to Chief Two Trees.

I invite you to become the source of hope in your life. Be the abundant spring. In the next chapters we will journey step by step together to discover and harvest the gifts of your spring of H.O.P.E. in your own life.

CHAPTER 6

The Energy of Hope

I was a cheerleader in high school and in college. I have been somewhat embarrassed to admit it, because cheerleaders have been much maligned as "eye candy" and shallow beneficiaries of popularity. But I loved being a cheerleader—not only cheering the team, but also teaching the crowds in the bleachers words of unity. It surprised me to realize recently that my job as a cheerleader was to inspire hope. Hope made the fans feel alive and created real, palpable energy. Hope infected the team with courage, resilience, and power. Skill was essential, but given evenly matched teams, hope could make the difference between winning and losing.

Through the years I have seen many individuals who were wounded or broken or had lost their way in life. Their mental, physical, or spiritual well-being had been crushed in some way. The only thing I could give them was hope. Hope is strength. Whether as a professor, pastor, counselor, author, or speaker, I have remained a cheerleader, inviting students, parishioners, clients, and others to be inspired, to believe in something beyond what they could see. In this chapter, I hope to share some of this hope energy with you.

HOPE AND ENERGY

Hope is pure energy. Energy is the fundamental element of the universe. Energy is any source of usable power. Energy is the ability to make something happen. Energy is the capacity for activity.

Cultures from around the world have similar descriptions for energy. Energy in the West is described as vigor, life, spirit, passion, and power. The Hindus call vital energy *prana*. The Hebrew name for vital energy is *ruah*. The Chinese call energy *chi*.

Prana is physical, mental, and spiritual energy in Hinduism—the fundamental energy and source of all knowledge. Hindus believe that when we practice yoga, our energy increases and improves our mental, physical, and spiritual health. The ability for you to cultivate, move, and grow this energy is essential.

Chi, in Eastern medicine, is the vital energy that flows through and connects all of the organs and systems of your body. Health means this energy is in balance. Energy facilitates our cells communicating to one another. Hope is a source of energy. The minute your mind plants the seeds of hope within you, a powerful healing energy is born. Just like gravity, hope is a force of physics and spirituality. Hope is a constant flow of energy that begins in the mind, grows in the soul, and actually changes the chemicals in our bodies. You can learn how to find ways to nourish and increase this flow of hope energy in your life. Do your own quick experiment with hope. Close your eyes, take a deep cleansing breath, and hope for something you want or need. Hope for a new love, more money, getting a degree, better health, or more peace in your life. Do you notice your heart rate changing, your mouth turning upward and beginning to smile, and your energy changing? You are experiencing the miraculous healing power of hope energy.

Where do you find the sources of hope in your own life? You can increase your hope by associating with hopeful people, spending time in nature, or reading inspirational books.

WHAT HOPE ENERGY CAN CREATE

Hope energy glues us together. As we have witnessed during political elections, hope is the glue that brings a group of different people together to promote solidarity. The candidate becomes the glue of hope that keeps them focused on winning, no matter what their differences are.

Hope energy unites us. There was just a $200 million lottery in Georgia. The nurses working in my husband's office each put in one dollar to buy a lottery ticket together. Each night over dinner he talked about the feverish level of the energy of hope that was evident in his office. The women began sharing in deeper and more profound ways. Susan said she had always wanted to have an education, and she wanted to get a degree. Eleanor's husband died years ago, and she would love to fix the leak in her roof. Sharing a dream of hope became a powerful energy that created vulnerability, intimacy, productivity, and a palpable increase in energy.

Hope energy heals. My husband, daughter, and I are all involved with patients on a regular basis, many with challenging diseases, dilemmas, and stressors. The hopeful patients are not only a true pleasure to work with, but they also create an energy that exudes through every facet of their treatment.

As Peter walks into chemotherapy he brings flowers to the nurses and puts his headphones on to listen to his guided imagery tape telling him about hope and healing. Peter experiences less nausea and actually is grateful to all the staff for helping to heal him. His hope infects these loving health-care professionals and gives them hope that they in turn spread to other patients and themselves.

Hope energy propels us to success. Laura wanted to take over as the senior manager of her consulting company. When she started her job, her boss advised her to be hopeful and focus on her goals, and she could someday be the senior manager. The day she was called in to receive her promotion to senior manager, her boss reminded her of her infectious energy of hope, which had changed the entire atmosphere at their office, making everyone more productive and happy.

Hope energy creates leaders. A leader inspires others to greater creativity, productivity, and happiness. Justin is the basketball coach at a local high school. Recently I went to a game coached by Justin and talked to some of his players. One player glowed when he talked about Coach Justin. "I got a scholarship to attend this private high school. I came from an inner-city school that was really tough. From the first day at practice Coach Justin changed my life. He taught me to hope for things I never dreamed possible. Coach looked into my eyes and told me I would be a college star player someday. From that day on I have focused on my grades, staying away from bad influences, and l live in the hope of being a college basketball player someday." The hope of one coach can affect the lives of untold young people.

Hope energy fuels love. Two people look into each other's eyes and promise to love and care for each other until their death. Love is rooted in the energy of hope. Through sickness and health, through wealth and poverty, the energy of hope is the guiding light like a lighthouse that lights the way to a deeper and more profound love. After thirty-five years of marriage, I can truly say that in the most difficult times of our marriage, hope was the energy that carried us through to the other side.

Hope energy translates to true happiness. Passion, vigor, and love are energies that can create true happiness in your life. Donna, a farmer who lives down the road from us, lost her husband a few years ago. She was left with a huge amount of debt on the farm, which was left in a state of disrepair. Farmwork is hard and can be risky with the volatility of commodity prices. But rain, sleet, snow, or drought, you can drive by Donna's farm and see her joyfully turn toward your truck with a wave and a smile of joy and hope on her face. She is always one of the first ones to our farm when we lose a horse or suffer from a farm loss. She infects all of us with her enormous power of hope that drives her happiness.

Hope energy drives social justice. Whether we fight apartheid, genocide, or any other form of oppression, the energy of hope drives us to the action of social justice. Many years ago I was involved in the struggle to pass the Equal Rights Amendment. There were five of us women on the team who headed across Georgia to lecture and teach about why we needed to pass the Equal Rights Amendment. We were on fire with the passionate energy of hope to move our country to a place where, regardless of gender, every American had equal rights under the law. Hope is the breath of life in all social justice movements.

Bishop Desmond Tutu was my professor at Emory. I will never forget the enormous energy of hope Bishop Tutu embodied in his victorious fight against apartheid. The energy of hope led Dr. Martin Luther King Jr. as he marched to Selma, and the energy of hope held the light for Nelson Mandela during his twenty-seven-year imprisonment.

WHY WE NEED HOPE ENERGY AND HOW TO GET IT

Our current lifestyle is literally killing us. The World Health Organization says that depression is the leading cause of disability in the world. By 2020 depression will be a leading cause of death and disability in the world, second only to heart disease. Each year about 850,000 lives are lost to suicide driven by depression.

Hope is the difference between chronic depression and a temporary setback. Whether you are struggling with a disease, are unemployed, or feel stressed out or lonely, stop right now and plant the seed of hope. Hope is the sign of a new beginning. It's anticipating the best instead of the worst, opening the window even though it might rain later. Hope has everything to do with happiness. Hope is believing you can have what you desire.

Have you ever tried to put your feet in a pair of your old shoes and you couldn't get your heel in the shoe? You had outgrown them, and there was no turning back. That's where you are now. Your lifestyle won't work the way it did before, because you now know the truth. Hope, like energy, transforms things, as great leaders and healers know.

When I made a list of the people I admired most in the world and in history—Mahatma Gandhi, Bishop Desmond Tutu, His Holiness the Dalai Lama, Thich Nhat Hanh, St. Francis of Assisi, Mother Teresa, Jane Goodall—the common thread was uncommon hope. Later I realized that each letter of the word *hope* stood for a trait that these people had in common: Honesty, Optimism, Perseverance, and En-joy. Every great person on my list was committed to honesty and inherently optimistic. Every obstacle became an opportunity that afforded their greatness. Perseverance ran through their blood, attached to every molecule of their hemoglobin, resulting in resilience. Each person I studied had overcome innumerable challenges throughout their lives. Finally, each person seemed filled with a mysterious sense of joy and wonder.

Hope has provided the Four Commitments to which I have dedicated my life. My happiness and all my successes are rooted in practicing these commitments. You, too, can be filled up and carried on your life's journey by committing to the fourfold path of H.O.P.E.: Honesty, Optimism, Perseverance, and En-Joy. After untold years of education, training, and experience, I have discovered that rooting your life in H.O.P.E. creates health, happiness, and success for an extraordinary life. Every culture, spirituality, and religion extols the power of this path.

THE FOUR COMMITMENTS

What is a commitment? It sounds like a commandment, which makes us think of the "Big Ten" on stone tablets. A commandment is something someone else tells you to do. But a commitment is personal. It springs from the depths of your soul. It is an intention that you follow through on, a promise that is more than a pledge.

A commitment is an action. It's not something you're going to do tomorrow. It is something you live today. It is an emotional and intellectual binding to a cause, principle, or purpose. A commitment is something solid you can count on. To commit is to believe what you do today affects the future.

These are the Four Commitments, the foundation for an extraordinary life of freedom, happiness, and peace for you, your family, and society.

- **HONESTY: The First Commitment**
  Aware of the suffering caused by lies, deceit, and dishonesty, I am committed to practicing HONESTY in every facet of my life.

- **OPTIMISM: The Second Commitment**
  Aware of the suffering caused by pessimism, negativity, and hopelessness, I am committed to practicing OPTIMISM in every facet of my life.

- **PERSEVERANCE: The Third Commitment**
  Aware of the suffering caused by apathy, impatience, and indifference, I am committed to practicing PERSEVERANCE in every facet of my life.

- **EN-JOY: The Fourth Commitment**
  Aware of the suffering caused by anger, violence, and grief, I am committed to cultivating JOY in every facet of my life.

There are no secret potions, mysterious formulas, or clandestine destinations you must visit to create the extraordinary life you desire. Simply practice incorporating the Four Commitments into all facets of your daily life: with your self, the Divine, your partner, your family, your workplace, and your community. This acronym, H.O.P.E., will lead you home like a light left on in the window at night.

H.O.P.E.

H is for honesty. Whatever you do, be honest with yourself. I can't tell you how many individuals I have seen who wasted my time and theirs by not being honest about who they were, what they wanted, or what they had done. When you are honest about your life, you have integrity. Honesty is a virtue that is the core of true greatness.

Be honest about where you are now, where you want to go, and why you aren't choosing to be there. People who do not live their truth experience tremendous stress, and research tells us about the health outcomes of dishonest lives. Learn how to live your true, honest life.

0 is for optimism. Every obstacle is an opportunity. Life is fraught with immense opportunities for growth that we initially perceive as obstacles. You may be living your life saying you didn't get an education or money or the life you want because of this and that obstacle. This means you have experienced the obstacles in your life as blocks, barriers, obstructions, or deterrents.

I challenge you to shift your thinking today. From now on, no matter what happens that seems like it is an obstacle, immediately say, "Well, isn't this an interesting opportunity for my growth? I can choose what is best for me in this opportunity, because I am grounded in the Four Commitments and feel confident and strong." When you stop perceiving your life as a series of paralyzing obstacles and understand it as a nonstop stream of opportunities (a chance for advancement, an opening, a favorable condition), you generate the energy to fuel a life of real happiness.

P is for perseverance. Introducing anything new into your busy life is not easy, and this is why perseverance is essential as you begin to live your new lifestyle grounded in the Four Commitments. When you choose to persevere, you are living with purpose, determination, endurance, and resolution. Anything life-changing that has ever happened in this world has happened because of perseverance.

Let's say you decide that the family is going to take walks three times a week for your family exercise, and your two children are not happy with your decision. They begin to pout and say nasty things, hoping you will give up. You must practice perseverance. Post the days and times of the walks on the refrigerator and expect everyone to meet at the garage. Make a decision and be determined and resolute. Learn new tools on how to persevere in any situation. Practicing perseverance promotes consistent energy flow.

E is for en-joy. Enjoy your wondrous life. Live in joy, love, happiness, and health. When you really enjoy your life, you will begin to savor, appreciate, and cherish your fragile, fleeting life. Treasure every breath, every relationship, every sunrise, and every sunset of your life. Enjoy means "in joy." Your purpose in this life is to live in joy. There are many ways to learn how to incorporate more joy and happiness into your life, and you will learn those here.

If you have ever known a person going through intensive cancer treatment who has a glow despite her pain; if you have ever nursed an animal, plant, or person back to health; if you have ever lived through a situation that demanded more strength than you thought you could muster—you have known hope as your companion.

My wish for you is that you can choose hope and move past any hopelessness or despair. Hope is the twin of happiness. Begin to close the door on feelings of powerlessness, disorientation, confusion, anger, sadness, depression, worry, and stress. Every moment is new, whether practicing H.O.P.E. with your self, the Divine, your partner, your family, at work, or in your community.

Like an underground spring, hope is waiting to bubble up and flow through your life. Tap it with your intention. Feel its power. Fuel it with honesty, optimism, perseverance, and joy. The source is already within you.

The next chapters of this book will lead you through this life-changing journey. Each aspect of H.O.P.E.—honesty, optimism, perseverance, and en-joy—will teach you how to live an extraordinary life of happiness and meaning.

CHAPTER 7

Honesty: The First Commitment

The Power of Truth

> **AWARE OF THE SUFFERING CAUSED BY LIES, DECEIT, AND DISHONESTY, I AM COMMITTED TO PRACTICING HONESTY IN EVERY FACET OF MY LIFE.**

There is a saying in twelve-step programs: "You're only as sick as your secrets." When I was a child, my life was full of secrets; our family was plagued by an epidemic of dishonesty that made us all sick. We had one identity in public—well-dressed children of Mr. and Ms. Hall, a handsome and successful couple. Inside the walls of our house, however, my father's erratic, violent behavior would strike with the force of lightning crackling down a dry tree trunk, creating wildfires that took weeks to burn out.

No one else in our town could have pictured my father sitting in his recliner in front of the TV with a revolver on the TV tray, drinking a Carling Black Label beer, watching Billy Graham, and cursing at us to listen to Graham's message of redemption. After Billy Graham's crusade, my mother would shepherd us into the next room to get on our knees under the crucifix of Jesus to say the rosary for the suffering people of the world.

Ashamed and terrified of my alcoholic father, I tried to escape from the truth at every opportunity. I would climb the big oak tree in our yard and look down on the chaos as if it were an evil fairy tale I had landed in by accident.

After I left the madness of that home, I promised myself that I would never speak of it. I created a life of nonviolence, incorporating my passion to care for suffering humans and animals. I learned to cover my unspeakable secrets with the beautiful bandages of wealth, power, and privilege. Thank God many wondrous therapists, healers, teachers, and friends taught me to face the horrors of my past and embrace a life of honesty and truth. No matter how much good I was doing in the world, I was not being honest with myself when I covered up my past.

My story is not unusual. We live in a culture of dishonesty, in a time of lies. Many of us questioned our government's honesty after the faulty and distorted intelligence that led us into our disastrous war with Iraq. Corporations like Enron, Tyco, Bear Stearns investment bankers, and AIG Insurance betrayed our trust and wounded our belief in fair business practices. Food manufacturers have allowed tainted products to be sold in markets around the world. Banks have eaten up our homes. Teachers are plagued with teens plagiarizing information and purchasing papers on the Internet. Our government and corporations have been dishonest about global warming and have actually falsified documents proving how quickly our planet is dying. The Catholic Church has been dishonest about sexual predators who have destroyed the lives of innocent children. Mothers and fathers worry about the honesty of their children and install computer programs and video monitors to track their recreational pursuits. And people continue to betray and divorce each other despite solemn marriage vows.

Dishonesty is an epidemic that we have become so accustomed to that we have accepted and integrated its distortions into our daily lives, poisoning our relationships and our jobs and damming the flow of our spiritual lives. We can neither shine a light nor stand in someone else's light when we are in a perpetual state of hiding from others and ourselves.

We lie when we are afraid of what others will think. We lie to try to manage situations that are out of control, which inevitably spin further out of control. With each lie, the fear of being found out grows and more lies are required. We have to remember what we said and to whom we said it as we swirl into this destructive and exhausting pattern. When we try to hold back the truth, which naturally bubbles from the source, we divert the course of nature.

What has happened to us? Where have we lost our way?

To be honest is to have integrity, to be genuine and sincere, incorruptible, good, heartfelt, and natural. You are created to live out these magnificent words in your everyday life, inhale and exhale them with every breath, pour them into your children, channel them into your career, prayers, and dreams. Please repeat this litany of beautiful words out loud to remind your self of what honesty is. Say, "I am genuine, sincere, incorruptible, good, heartfelt, and natural. I am honest."

Think of the great leaders and their words of truth that live in our hearts and minds: Jesus, Buddha, Lao Tzu, Abraham Lincoln, Mother Teresa, Bishop Desmond Tutu, Mahatma Gandhi, Martin Luther King Jr., Maya Angelou, Henry David Thoreau, Ralph Waldo Emerson, and Chief Seattle to name a few.

Abraham Lincoln was known as "Honest Abe." Chief Seattle said, "My honest words are like the stars that never change," and "An honest heart possesses a kingdom." "Rather than love, than money, than fame, give me truth," said Thoreau. Mahatma Gandhi said, "There is no god higher than truth." Jesus said, "You will know the truth, and the truth shall make you free." "Truth is the property of no individual, but is the treasure of all men," stated Emerson. In the grips of great injustice, Martin Luther King Jr. said, "I believe that unarmed truth and unconditional love will have the final word in reality," and Bishop Desmond Tutu said, "I never doubted that ultimately we were going to be free, because ultimately, I knew there was no way in which a lie could prevail over the truth."

Speaking the truth has an energy and life of its own; honesty can inspire generations of millions of human beings. I believe when you are honest, you are one with the Divine energy and propelled into a holy realm.

The truth heals and lies destroy. Lies or dishonesty eat away at the person who tells them and dismantle all elements of our existence. Telling a lie is like volunteering for prison. You live a life of bondage when you live dishonestly. Living dishonestly causes exhaustion. Truth creates freedom and energy for the mind, body, and soul.

Do this exercise for a minute. Say something honest about yourself and then repeat it again. Now say something dishonest about yourself and repeat it. Do you notice a change not only in your emotions but also in your energy? When you are dishonest your eyes may blink, your blood pressure may change, and your heart may change its rhythm.

You may believe living dishonestly is justified by your economic situation and that you can change later in life when your circumstances change. Just remember, the longer you avoid the truth, the greater price you will pay. When we avoid the truth about a relationship, the result can be infidelity or divorce. When we avoid the truth about our health, the result can be disease. When we avoid the truth about evil or oppression in our countries, it can result in wars. There is an old saying that I love: "Pay now or pay later." When you pay later, there are more consequences for your choices.

A fundamental element of psychotherapeutic counseling is to discover the truth about the clients or patient's life. Different schools of psychology use various methods of discovery to aid the patients in disclosing the truth of their life. The counselor becomes the encourager or "cheerleader" as the patients explore their past and present life to uproot their conscious and unconscious secrets and lies. The belief system is, simply put, "The truth will set you free."

When we have lived a life of dishonesty, either consciously or unconsciously, we need lots of support to help us gain the courage to finally tell the truth. This has been my experience with both my own therapy and doing counseling with others for many years. The more a client continues to tell the truth, live the truth, and believe in the truth, the healthier and stronger they become mentally, physically, and spiritually.

As always, an accessible source of honesty and truth for me was nature. When I was a child, in times of confusion nature was the place where the power of truth resided. A rose is always a rose. Our horse always lives its truth as a horse. The seasons are pure and true. Our dog consistently lives the true life of a dog. No lies, manipulations, or confusion.

To explore and appreciate honesty, begin with a simple walk in nature. There is tremendous balance, power, and flow in the truth of nature. Another healing place to discover honesty is any twelve-step program, whether it is Alcoholics Anonymous, Al-Anon, Narcotics Anonymous, Overeaters Anonymous, or any similar program. It is a spiritual experience to witness the power of truth in community.

Beginning a regular spiritual practice is a step to discovering the truth of who you are and why you are here. Meditation is a simple spiritual practice that benefits your mental, physical, and spiritual health. You can find a meditation teacher in your community or take a class online.

As a spiritual director it has always been gratifying to observe clients and patients begin their paths to embracing honesty to heal their lives. When we live our truth we become whole. Energy flows through us into the world, and we become a beacon of light, love, and hope in our world.

"Truth is a Divine unfolding of unwavering commandments that have eternal reverberations," said Mahatma Gandhi, and to that I say Amen.

Honesty pervades every facet of your life; your self, your marriage, your relationship with the Divine, at work, in your family, and in your community. The next chapters will address each part of your life to give you specific information to enrich your life.

CHAPTER 8

Honesty with My Self

> **AWARE OF THE SUFFERING CAUSED BY LIES, DECEIT, AND DISHONESTY, I AM COMMITTED TO HONESTY WITH MY SELF.**

I grew up in the Catholic Church, and honesty is one of the core values of the Catholic religion. Not being honest or telling a lie is considered a sin. There are two types of sins in the Catholic Church: mortal and venial sins. Mortal sins are the big ones, like killing someone or stealing something. Venial sins are smaller, including the little lies we tell. I remember saying I was sorry for telling my mom a lie about my girlfriend or a phone call or an outfit I wore that she didn't know about. I always felt guilty, but the Church had the sacrament of reconciliation. I visited the confessional once a week and would include Acts of Contrition during my nightly prayers. Each time I asked for forgiveness, I would promise to never lie or be dishonest again.

Like most of us, I repeated a little lie within twenty-four hours of my confession. These I considered little survival lies to my parents.

But no matter how I tried to justify them, they always bothered me. I felt evil when I told lies to my parents or teachers. Yet then, as today, teenage honesty seemed like a relative commodity. After all, my friends were doing it. But why did I always feel so guilty?

The reason I felt so guilty is because there is a set of ethics and morals that is codified in our religions and evidenced in most cultures. The Ten Commandments are found in most religions of the world in some form. The Ninth Commandment is "Do not bear false witness," which in modern words is "Do not lie!"

How many of us have heard the threat from our parents in our homes: "If I catch you lying…"? In school it was one of the primary rules of the educational process: "Do not lie, cheat, or steal." In our religious studies classes at church there was a constant reverberating theme of "Don't lie. No matter what, tell the truth." There was not one segment of my childhood that condoned not telling the truth. When I told a little white lie, every cell of my body shook on some level saying, "You know better, don't do it."

The reason I tell this story about my own experience with truth telling and lying is because I believe my primary experiences with not being honest are pretty universal. The small, shady childhood lies began because I wanted to be loved and didn't want to disappoint my parents and authority figures. Most kids lie, and teenage lies are quite common. It is when we move from the teenage phase of development into adulthood that dishonesty seriously erodes our ability to live happily. These childhood behavior patterns can evolve into permanent, destructive pathological patterns.

Most of us didn't tell our parents everything that happened at college or during our early years of independence in our twenties. We did some pretty pathetic things to ourselves and others learning to be adults: the drunken parties, the bad people we dated, the nights we don't remember, the tests we cheated on, the cars we wrecked, and the list goes on and on.

Not being honest or living our truth destroys our self-esteem. It is like building our lives on unstable drifting sand instead of the solid rock of truth. Where do you draw the line between childhood lies and serial lying as an adult?

One indicator is our stress level and severity of depression. Are these isolated episodes or ongoing states of being? Serenity and honesty are woven together, inextricably linked. Peace of mind comes only when we live honest lives.

What we desire above all things is a sense of peace and serenity. We experience moments of peace and serenity at the intimate times in our lives: when you love someone, sit in nature, meditate, pet your dog or cat, work in your garden, listen to great music, or ride your horse. In that magnificent space in time, we experience that sacred moment of serenity. We seek serenity in our lives, but this holy experience becomes elusive when we live busy, chaotic lives that we invent to please those we love and to appease the world.

Honesty is born in our thoughts. Our thoughts are the seeds to grow an honest life. Each thought we think has repercussions in the world. From our thoughts unfold words and actions. Lying can begin simply.

For example, you feel insecure because you don't have a college degree. You tell others that you have a college degree because you feel so ashamed not to have a degree. A person in the Starbucks line sees you in an Ohio State shirt and asks you if you went to Ohio State. You say yes. You both smile and she says, "Go Buckeyes." You pick up your coffee and go to the car and feel a little guilty, but then you tell yourself, oh, that was just a little white lie. The next move may be to lie on a resume. Once you have told a lie, it becomes easier to keep being dishonest.

But with every lie, there is an irritation, a shaming that occurs. Eventually, you lose your sense of peace and serenity and self-respect.

We sabotage our lives when we do not live honestly. We create suffering for ourselves and others when we live with secrets. We may be being dishonest about our sexuality. Some of the most painful family situations I have ever experienced were when someone in a family was not honest about their sexuality and lived a lie in the family. But many families are not supportive about homosexuality, and therefore the way many survive is by not telling the truth about who they really are.

Is it worth it to lie even in that situation? It depends on if mere survival is your goal. It may be your short-term goal, but a longer-term goal should be to thrive, to tear down all the dams you have built over and over to hold back the artificial lakes of lies you have told. Open the floodgates. There will be tears, but as long as they spring from the source of your soul, the depths of who you really are, your natural wellspring of goodness and integrity will bubble up.

I am known for being painfully honest. Many years ago I chose to live with integrity and to speak the truth. The more you commit to living the truth and always speaking honestly, the more freedom, power, and courage you will experience.

Sit in silence with yourself in a peaceful place. Be aware of your thoughts, worries, or concerns as they float up in your mind in your silence.

- **What information is coming out of your mind and soul?**
- **Is it busy talk without much substance?**

- **What is the truth about your soul when you enter the sacred silence?**
- **Are you riddled with fears, worries, or depression?**
- **Or are you connected to love, energy, and hope in your silence?**
- **What is the truth of your life?**

Visit nature on a regular basis or create a garden in your yard. Tending to your garden or regularly visiting nature will give you much insight to your truth about life. Are you peaceful, frustrated, angry, or distracted? Do you feel at one with nature and celebrate the scent of the wind and cherish the songs of the birds and the rustling of the trees? Nature is a powerful rhythm of energy that can give you lots of information about your life.

A journal is a great source of honesty and truth. Writing regularly and intimately can reveal the person living within you that you are going to love. Journaling is a fascinating healing process that over time will be a chronicle of your life.

Go to your bathroom mirror and take off your clothes. What do you think about your body? Are you judgmental and critical, or are you compassionate, accepting, and loving of your precious body? Be honest about how you feel. Many of us have learned to hate our bodies, and very few of us have a healthy mind-set about our physical bodies. Remember your body is the map of your life. Every scar, wrinkle, or stretch mark is a story of your sacred journey. If you experience judgment about your body, create a loving affirmation and be grateful for this miraculous vehicle that is giving you this life experience.

Be honest about your mental status. Have you been feeling depressed, sad, or slow? Have you been stressed out, and is the anxiety getting more difficult to manage each day? Do an honesty and truth inventory of your life, mental, physical, and spiritual. Explore the truth of your relationships.

You can never experience true serenity without honesty. Be honest with yourself, and your light and energy will flow naturally and abundantly into the world.

BEGIN TODAY

What is my excuse for not practicing honesty with my self?

Ask *Your Self*

What is the one thing I must face in my life?

Tell *Your Self*

My honesty creates peace, serenity, and love in the world.

Give *Your Self*

Join a meditation or yoga class to plant the seed of honesty in your life.

CHAPTER 9

Honesty with the Divine

> **AWARE OF THE SUFFERING CAUSED BY LIES, DECEIT, AND DISHONESTY, I AM COMMITTED TO HONESTY WITH THE DIVINE.**

One day many years ago I was having lunch with a good friend of mine who is a rabbi. I told Rabbi Levy about the anger that had been simmering in me about God since childhood. I said I was afraid of what could happen if I unleashed my rage to God.

He dropped his fork and belly laughed. He said, "I thought you had read the Psalms and the Bible."

"Yes, I have read them."

Rabbi Levy leaned over his plate and said, "These people in the Bible are really angry with God for the death, famine, and losses of their life. They let God have it! Then in the next line they would sing praises to God. God isn't a wimp. Get angry with God. Free yourself. Go home to your farm, go out into the pasture, and let God have your forty years of anger. After you do this, call me and we'll have lunch again and talk."

The weekend after our lunch I went to the pasture with my fear, anger, and rage all rooted deep within my soul for many years. I started in a small whisper with a list of complaints that began with my father's abuse, my mother's suffering, and on to an inventory of the many years of anger. That whisper grew to a loud yell. Before I knew it, the ranting and crying ended with my body falling into the green grass in exhaustion.

I waited for lightning to strike me, thunder to roll in, or me to just die lying there. But instead the birds were singing, the sun was shining, the horses were grazing a few feet from me, and the world was at peace. Rabbi Levy was right. I was brutally honest with the Divine for the first time in my existence, and all was well.

Fear and *love* are the two words I would use to describe my relationship with the Divine for the first forty years of my life. Growing up Catholic I remember my first communion and the tremendous devotion and love in my soul for God on that day of my life. Nature was the place where I nourished that love and immersed myself into the essence of the Divine. This love and devotion has been the taproot of my life and has continued to grow.

There was also the dark side of my relationship with the Divine. Most of my life I was afraid to confront this omnipotent Divine power about my rage over the violence and injustice I had to endure and survive in my childhood. I was afraid something horrible would happen to my family or me.

My theology changed over time, and I stopped believing in this anthropomorphic God, a God with human emotions who could get angry or love. The longer I lived in nature, the more I shifted my belief to panentheism, a belief that God exists and interpenetrates every part of nature and exists beyond nature as well—the belief that God is in everything in creation, that there is not a God "out there." I began to experience the Divine in a flower, a dog, a sunset, or a rainstorm. As my experience of this divinity in all creation grew, I felt a communion with the Divine in everything I did in life.

Being totally honest with the Divine was the first step of my being able to develop an entirely new construct of what the Divine is in my life. How many of us live in our birth religions and fear confronting aspects of God we dislike or don't believe?

I saw David as a client for a couple of years. He lived in a constant state of struggle with his religion and God. He grew up Southern Baptist but grew to disagree with many of the policies of the church, such as the Southern Baptist Convention's authority, sexual preference issues, women not being ordained, and many more. His anger had grown to a fever pitch, but he could not leave the church of his Southern religious family because of his children and other family ties to the church. He would sit in my office and rant about his rage about the Baptist Church for an hour, then get up and leave.

This continued for some time until David came to the realization that the honest thing to do would be to develop a meaningful spiritual relationship with the Divine beyond organized religion. The institution was not prohibiting him from pursuing his spiritual quest. He began centering prayer, joined an interfaith spirituality study group, and took a night class on world religions. David cultivated a very deep spiritual life with lots of support from new friends. He experiences a new sense of peace and love these days.

When you are connected or experience communion with the Holy, you experience peace and serenity. If you are living a life of dishonesty or lies, you cannot have this holy experience with the Divine. All religions and spiritualities hold the belief that God is truth.

Mahatma Gandhi created a term he referred to as *Satyagraha. Satya* means "truth." *Graha* is the force, or "soul force," and Divine energy that propel the truth. Gandhi believed that when a person tells the truth, there is a Divine energy that drives the truth into our hearts and minds. Being honest, telling the truth, creates an energy that is holy and lives past us and beyond us. There is energy in truth, a power, an authority and autonomy that is the essence of truth. When Gandhi talked about essential qualities of character, the first and most important quality is honesty. He believed you must speak and live honestly: "God is truth, so we live in God when we live truth."

Twelve-step programs, such as Alcoholics Anonymous, Narcotics Anonymous, and others, are founded in the requirement that one must believe that only a greater power of truth, your Higher Power, can restore one to sanity or health. The second step of the twelve-step program is "Come to believe that a Power greater than ourselves could restore us to sanity." Whatever our affliction or addiction may be, the source of our woundedness is rooted in our dishonesty about the way we are living our lives.

The healing power of truth is seen in step five of the twelve steps: "Admit to God [or your Higher Power], to ourselves, and to another human being the exact nature of our wrongs." This means tell the truth. Surrender, be honest, and tell the truth about your life. For many this is the first time that they have the courage and support to be honest about their lives and the choices they have made. The twelve-step program is all about telling the truth and beginning to live an honest life of integrity with the connection of your Higher Power, or the Divine.

We know what truth and honesty are, but we cannot always practice them on our own. Sometimes we have to ask for help from a Higher Power, God, religion, or various spiritual entities.

We live in a diverse global world with our citizens practicing a wide variety of world religions. What do you know about how various religions experience the Divine in their dogma, doctrine, or sacred texts? Consider taking a world religion class at a local community college, or purchase a world religion book and explore other religions of the world.

One of the greatest joys of my professional career was teaching world religions at a local college. Students from a variety of religions from all over the country attended my classes with great curiosity and fascination. Every class I taught transformed my life and the lives of the students.

How much do you know about your birth religion? If you were born Jewish, Christian, Muslim, or Taoist, how much do you really know about the tenets of your religion? I taught Emory seminary students training to be ordained ministers in a variety of Christian denominations, and most of them had never known the history of the early Christian Church. Most of the students were shocked to discover the rich history of their faith.

Discover the Divine in new ways. If you have not listened to the Divine in the silence of meditation, this could be the time to take a meditation class. Many find new meaning with the Divine through music or art. I took an amazing iconography class that challenged my previous experience of the Divine. I have studied with shamans in the midst of nature, and my concept of the Divine expanded beyond anything I would have imagined. I invite you to explore the many paths to the Divine. Your journey will be exciting, and you will be amazed to discover the wondrous other souls on a similar rich path to an extraordinary life.

We each have a source or spring of our own, but to replenish it and keep it moving on a path we need to connect with the Divine, where there is always an abundance of holy water to both soothe and freshen.

BEGIN TODAY

What is my excuse for not practicing honesty with the Divine?

Ask *Your Self*

How can I experience the Divine in a new way?

Tell *Your Self*

Divine energy flows through me as I live honestly each day.

Give *Your Self*

Explore a different religion or spirituality that interests you.

CHAPTER 10

Honesty with My Partner

AWARE OF THE SUFFERING CAUSED BY LIES, DECEIT, AND DISHONESTY, I AM COMMITTED TO PRACTICING HONESTY WITH MY PARTNER.

"Do you take this person from this day forward, for better, for worse, for richer, for poorer, in sickness and in health, to love and to cherish, until death do you part?" This is where the rubber meets the road. If you don't mean these vows, don't say them.

Over thirty years ago, I was a "runaway bride." The night before my wedding, I kept reading those words over and over again. The day of my wedding I came to the panicked conclusion that it would be dishonest for me to promise these words to another human being. How could I promise this virtuous oath until death do us part? I was only twenty-three years old. I loved Jim, but I was brutally honest about not knowing whether I could be with him our entire life.

I decided to jump ship and run away. Later in the day my mother sent a posse to round me up for the evening wedding, but to this day I never said "I do" to those words. At my wedding, when I stood in front of the priest after he read the vows, he kept telling me to say, "I do." The more he pressured me, the more the tears poured and the greater my resistance rose. Father Bill finally said "I do" for me. So here I am, living in sin for over thirty-five years.

The reason I tell this story is to make it clear that whatever you hold as truth is yours. Your integrity is sacred. It did not matter that the Church, society, and my family expected me to say these words. My own truth said no! My knowledge of marriage was based on that of my parents, which was a grisly experience. These two people had vowed to stay together, no matter what, "until death do us part." These traditional vows seemed like a jail sentence to me instead of a promise of love, life, and growth. Our experience of truth is informed by our own experiences.

This was the first profound moment of naked honesty with my husband. Unlike many men, my husband was enlightened enough to know my actions were not about him. This was the defining incident that revealed what each of us valued. This incident provided a doorway for my husband and me to have a deeper level of truth and intimacy in our relationship. He experienced my power and boundaries as I experienced his compassion and respect for my choices. It was an incredible opportunity for us to root our relationship in honesty and integrity.

As a pastoral caregiver, I counseled couples before they married, and I listened and refereed after the marriage. Dishonesty is the rotten core of so many relationships. Too many women "settle" to get a man. Women believe there are too many women for the number of men, and they "sell out" to get a man. Yes, it is disgusting in this day and age, but it is a reality. I know women who are doctors, lawyers, professors, and other professionals who give up their values and their truth to have a partner. Socioeconomic class is no preventative for the plague of "settling."

Settling is when a person knowingly gives up truths that they value to keep or sustain a relationship. Please wake up and realize that you are living a lie when you are desperate for a relationship and give up the gift of *you* for the desires of someone else. A few signs of knowing that you are settling for an inadequate relationship are when you have conflicting core values, when your partner does not respect you or your opinion, or when the other person continually makes important decisions without your consultation.

There is a myth that people believe. This myth says things will get better when you get married. If your partner is a liar, a drinker, a philanderer, or controlling, you may believe he or she will change for the better once you give that person your love and share your true self. Those of you reading this who partnered with this type of person know the truth. Things only get worse once you put that ring on your finger and say "until death do us part."

Give yourself the gift of life. Be your fully truthful, honest, whole self in your relationship with your significant other or spouse. Life is a rich adventure of love, passion, loss, and abundance that is best when it springs from honesty. Maintaining honesty in your relationship is a spiritual practice that must be tended to like a fragile garden. Weeds can pop up overnight, and it takes extreme vigilance to protect and nurture what is most important to you. I can assure you, it is worth every moment of tending.

Be honest, but also be kind. If you don't like his suit, be honest and kind. You can say something like, "I love you, but I don't think that suit makes you look as good as you could look. What do you think?" Be honest about not liking jewelry or gifts you receive. Believe me, I have been through this myself. Just sit down and tell the other person you love him or her, but this gift is not your taste. Your partner spent lots of money on a gift and wants it to be something you will wear or love. Ask to be a part of gift choices so it will really be something you love and will wear for a lifetime. I was honest many years ago with my husband. I told him our tastes in clothes and jewelry were totally different. If he wanted me to be happy and wear his gifts, I would have to choose my own jewelry and clothes. This took the pressure off him, and we have built on this honesty and been very happy with our gift-giving decisions our entire marriage.

Tending is a tender term, and that is how we have to treat this holy state of union that can make us whole. Just as a master gardener knows exactly how to tend to her garden, we must learn how to tend to our fragile sacred union. Tending is a daily loving, touching process of growing awareness of each other's needs and dreams. Tending is an ancient practice of love. Tending to your union will keep your love and commitment in balance and on track.

My own relationship has gotten off track many times in thirty-plus years. When we traced where and when the fissure began, it always led to a thread of dishonesty with each other. Honesty in a relationship is crucial. The pain of infidelity is incomparable and unfathomable. The only way out of this horrendous situation is pure honesty and truth.

As partners, you each have your own source, your own wellspring for filling up with energy and hope. Keeping things honest allows each of you to tend to your own self as well as your relationship.

One simple practice to remember for a healthy, honest relationship is to keep a date night once a week. This is the intimate time when each person is honest and fully present without distractions. The goal of this date is intimacy, no talking business. Schedule a once-a-week meeting for the business of your relationship and your lives. Every three or four months go away for at least one night with your partner.

This not only fosters intimacy but also displays to your children how much you are committed to, cherish, and respect your union. Touch is a magical and essential communication. Daily moments of touching, hugging, and kissing build confidence, honesty, and trust in your relationship. Touching also fosters play, which leads to sexuality.

Sex and intimacy are crucial for a good relationship. We sabotage our sexual relationships with too much work, too many distractions, and too much exhaustion. Sex is sacred and has to be intentionally kept on the front burner. Be honest about how you feel about sex. Some of the saddest relationships I have witnessed were those in which one or both of the partners were never honest about how they liked or disliked sex or certain sexual practices. These days pornography has crept into so many relationships and torn them apart. When men choose to watch pornography, in the beginning they may innocently ask their wives to watch it with them. This can lead to the wife participating in sexual activity she is not comfortable with and to not being honest about how she feels about it. So many women have ended up in my office with shame, anger, and low self-esteem because their sex life has spiraled into something disgusting and dirty, not sacred, holy, and nourishing. Never give away your self-respect and power.

Always be honest about what you value. If you cannot talk honestly about what you love and what you will not compromise in your relationship, find a counselor you both respect and trust. Every five years my husband and I go to a counselor to redo our commitment to each other, just like reenlisting in the army. We clear out our anger, frustrations, and work on better communication skills and intimacy. It feels like a spring house cleaning in our relationship. We want our relationship to stay vital, fresh, exciting, and rewarding. That takes intentional work.

A good relationship takes hard, diligent work and is pure gold. It is rooted in honesty and truth. It is never too late to plant the seeds of truth. Don't forget to water and tend them, for the fruit is truly sweet and nourishing.

BEGIN TODAY

What is my excuse for not being honest with my partner?

Ask *Your Self*

What one thing could I do to create more honesty in my relationship?

Tell *Your Self*

My relationship is rooted in honesty and respect.

Give *Your Self*

Get your calendar and schedule your weekly date night.

CHAPTER 11

Honesty with My Family

AWARE OF THE SUFFERING CAUSED BY LIES, DECEIT, AND DISHONESTY, I AM COMMITTED TO PRACTICING HONESTY WITH MY FAMILY.

I know about family secrets, shunning, and rejection. There were so many secrets in my family that living each day was like negotiating a fully loaded minefield.

As a child, I knew something was going on when my uncle used to visit from Arizona, but I couldn't put my finger on it.

Every time he would visit, my mother would become anxious and hypervigilant. My mother was always busy and distracted as she managed our home of seven children. But when Uncle Jerry visited, my mother's personality changed drastically.

I felt weird around him. He was creepy, so I tried to stay away from him. If I were in the kitchen alone, he would show up and put his hand on my back. If I were in the living room, he would suddenly appear and ask me if I wanted to take a walk. He gave me the willies, and I was terrified of him but couldn't understand why. I felt trapped with my confusing emotions about my uncle. Who could I tell about what I felt? He hadn't done anything to me, so what was I going to tell someone he did? It felt like "crazy making," so I tried to hide in my room or outside when Uncle Jerry visited.

It wasn't until many years later, when my cousin was visiting our family, that the secrets hidden for so long came to the surface. Connie had a couple glasses of wine, and the tears began to flow. She asked me if anything strange had happened to me when Uncle Jerry came to stay when I was a child. I told her how creepy he made me feel and that I was terrified of him for some reason.

She wiped the tears away from her cheeks and abruptly announced, "He molested me. From the time I was eight, he began to rub my back. Then I would be watching television, and he would pick me up and put me on his lap. Before I knew it he was taking me on walks with him, and on those walks he would touch me all over." Then she began to cry again. "I hate him, and I know he did it to others, so I am going around to all of our family, and I want the truth."

Connie and I went to my mother to tell the truth about Uncle Jerry. The words were not out of our mouths when she told me to be quiet and not tell anyone. She said this secret would destroy our family, and we should keep our mouths shut. I will always remember the betrayal I felt in that moment. A child molester in our family was a secret. The God in our religion tells us to be honest. Our parents are charged to protect their children, and we were being told to be silent and lie about a child molester who had caused massive suffering.

Uncovering lies, one at a time, is risky business. Once you know, it is hard not to tell, but it is equally difficult to continue to live the lie. I was the one who always spilled the beans and always got into trouble. I was the one who found out about the sexual dysfunction, the pregnancies, the violence, and the destructive addictions of the family. Most of us have enormous secrets in our families. Some of us look the other way, some of us become numb, some of us surrender to depression or anxiety disorders, some of us go mad, and some of us begin to entertain thoughts of suicide to survive the pain of these family secrets.

I wish we could stop the lie of keeping secrets to protect our fragile children. Children of any age can take the truth better than they can take a lie. Children are more resilient than we believe they are. A child can take any truth as long as it is told with love and support.

Family secrets are family lies. Dishonesty is not just what one says verbally, but also what is held in silence. I have always lived by the statement "Secrets kill and the truth heals." A family secret is like a hidden ticking bomb just waiting to explode. The family constructs a life around the impending time bomb. The family secret may be the adoption of a child or the sexuality of your favorite uncle or the rape of your mother or a mental illness or addiction in a family member.

Whatever the secret, it causes separation and suffering in a family. Children innately know when there is a lie in a family. There is an energy to a lie that each member of the family sidesteps in fear of an explosion.

One of the greatest fears of a family member is shunning. Shunning is an ancient practice that is still used today in many cultures, and humans have an innate fear of it. When a member of any group disagrees with the norms or the values of the family, the family may expel that person from the group. The Amish and other religions use this practice to maintain control of the group.

In the animal kingdom, shunning can mean certain death. When an animal becomes disabled in the wild, the herd will shun the animal, and the immune system of the shunned animal immediately changes.

The animal risks death in isolation. The animal may die, because in a state of isolation it loses the protection of the herd—or it may fall to predators in its weakened state. Research tells us that when humans are isolated or shunned by a group, our immune system starts to shut down. When a family lives with secrets or dishonesty, most of us will stay in our dysfunctional family because of the pain of shunning, rejection, and isolation.

Many of us will walk on eggshells to stay in a family of secrets and pain rather than suffer the consequences of rejection and abandonment. In some families it is very risky to tell the truth. We all want to be loved, accepted, and appreciated, especially by our families. When we begin to question our family values or our family's religion, we risk losing the adoring, accepting looks from those we love. We innately know this as small children. We begin to live secret lives and to keep the secrets of our own truths. Children become compliant for survival. They survive with the love and protection of their family, and without it they could die.

As parents it is our responsibility to teach our children that honesty and truth are the glue of a family. Honesty is the foundation of a healthy family's moral code. We have to create a family in which each member of the family feels safe being honest and revealing their truth.

If family members feel unsafe or the environment is unstable, it is almost impossible to foster the gift of honesty. To be completely honest means you are vulnerable and open.

I worked with a family who was struggling with how to be honest in a challenging situation in their family. Claire, their sixteen-year-old daughter, came to her parents and told them she had told a lie to the principal at her high school. She did not like some girls in one of her classes, so she went to the principal's office and told him she had mononucleosis and had to be out of school for a couple of weeks. She produced a note from her mother that said she had been taken to the doctor and diagnosed.

At the dinner table that night Claire felt so guilty she broke down and told her parents the lie she had told to Dr. Jackson, the principal of her school. After a long conversation Claire and her parents decided to go the next morning and tell Dr. Jackson the truth. They didn't know what the consequences would be, but they knew that honesty and living the truth were core family values for them.

The parents went with Claire to talk to the principal. Claire had panicked and reacted with a silly lie. Claire was an excellent student and had never been in trouble. Dr. Jackson recommended family counseling and told them how impressed he was that the entire family came in to be honest and face the consequences of Claire's actions.

The family grew even closer after this crisis. Claire appreciated that her parents not only encouraged her to face her lie but also wanted to go with her to support her in her honesty. It has been years since this incident with Claire. Claire is now a prestigious lawyer, and her family is incredibly close and loving.

There are simple ways to help develop honesty in your family. Research continues to reveal the positive psychological virtues fostered by simply eating dinner together as a family. You create a forum for the cultivation of honesty and vulnerability when you take the time and commitment to celebrate food and share stories with each other.

Each holiday is an opportunity to teach your children about the value of honesty. As you spend holiday time with other families, neighbors, and friends, you have the chance to observe, listen, and foster your children's honesty about their experiences. This can create the basis for a lifetime of rich, loving memories.

Many of us do not have a biological family rooted in honesty. We are then challenged to create a nonbiological family where we can live in honesty. You can seek family in your community through special interest groups such as animal rescue groups, twelve-step programs, yoga and meditation groups, or gardening enthusiasts. Celebrate holidays, rituals, birthdays and losses with your supportive family.

Anything is possible when we create a family environment where everyone is supported and loved in their journey to honesty and truth. Like an underground spring, the pressure is too great to keep it from spilling out sooner or later.

BEGIN TODAY

What is my excuse for not being honest with my family?

Ask *Your Self*

How can I set an example of honesty in our family?

Tell *Your Self*

My family is a safe, supportive place to be honest.

Give *Your Self*

Never keep family secrets.

Honesty with My Work

> **AWARE OF THE SUFFERING CAUSED BY LIES, DECEIT, AND DISHONESTY, I AM COMMITTED TO PRACTICING HONESTY WITH MY WORK.**

I gave a speech on stress and living a balanced life to a large organization a few years ago on a Wednesday. I flew back to Atlanta and walked into my office Thursday morning, and my publicist handed me a FedEx overnight package addressed to me.

I opened the package, and there was a letter from Angela, who had heard me speak the day before. She began the letter by telling me how much she enjoyed my speech. Angela went on to tell me that she wanted to be honest and offer me some feedback and suggestions for innovations she believed would change The Stress Institute.

She proceeded with some incredible insights and some tough criticisms straight from her heart. I was so impressed with her heartfelt honesty that I picked up the phone and called her immediately.

Angela became a part of our team and one of the greatest visionaries I have ever had the privilege of working with. All of our staff was drawn to her guidance, wisdom, and energy. She was a leader from the start and grew our companies in innovative and profitable projects.

It all started with her shocking, straightforward, bold honesty. I just loved it. That kind of honesty in a company feels like a cool breeze on your face, a warmed heart, and a beautiful sunrise all packaged together. Every day I looked forward to walking into our offices, and when I saw her emails, I immediately opened them with anticipation.

On the other hand, betrayal, anger, and sadness pop up for me when I think about moments of dishonesty I've faced in the office, such as finding pornography on one of my employees' computers, discovering charges at a liquor store on one of my credit cards used by an employee, hearing lies from staff about work never done, and more. Those of us who work in companies feel a stab through our hearts when we discover a trusted employee is dishonest or lies. It may take a day or a month or years, but I promise you this: in my experience of running many companies, dishonesty always shows up. Small company owners like myself consider employees as family. I still don't understand how people can look in the face of the person who loves and cares for the company, the person who signs their paychecks, and be dishonest.

Why wouldn't the workplace be the most dishonest place in our world these days? What kind of examples have we seen in recent years?

Do you believe that members of Congress, the lobbying groups in Washington, D.C., the groups involved in intelligence, or the White House are always honest with us? Lewis "Scooter" Libby, former chief of staff to Vice President Dick Cheney, was sentenced to prison for lying to investigators looking into the leak of a CIA operative's identity. Libby was convicted on four counts of a five-count indictment alleging perjury, obstruction of justice, and making false statements to FBI investigators. It is tragic when the citizens of a country cannot trust in the honesty of their government officials or the government itself. We need some cleaning up of the government and a new policy of honesty and integrity.

Our image of industry and corporate leaders has been tarnished as well. There has been a wave of prosecutions against business executives over the past years. We were awestruck by the dishonesty of Tyco's former CEO, Dennis Kozlowski, who looted $600 million from his company. The financial collapse, bankruptcy, and criminal trials surrounding Enron were astounding. This was not the dishonesty of just one CEO, but thirty-four criminal defendants. Yet those were small potatoes compared with what happened in 2008 with the bailouts of the auto and financial industries, when the financial disaster was attributed to greed and dishonesty. This total disregard for honest and ethical behavior began at the top, not with low-paid employees' pilfering.

These examples of dishonesty in our largest institutions are astonishing and sickening. We must require programs for institutions that instruct all personnel about the economic, emotional, and even physical benefits of honesty. Honesty is the source of positive self-esteem, a healthy ego, courage, and power.

Where dishonesty is part of the corporate culture, there will be significant negative costs associated with its practice in the workplace. You don't have to embezzle $600 million to be dishonest at work. How about lying about what time you got to work? What about sneaking out for thirty minutes while at work or playing an online game on your employer's time? How about calling in sick to work and lying about being ill? How about taking products home from work and justifying it by telling yourself how hard you work and that you deserve these stolen products?

The list of small dishonesties could go on for pages. But the truth is, you begin with the justification of dishonesty in the smallest of things, and then you grow numb to feeling guilty about being dishonest.

Nineteen percent of workers admitted they tell lies at the office once a week according to CareerBuilder.com's "Honesty in the Workplace" survey. Fifteen percent of workers reported they were caught in a lie at the office. Nearly one in four hiring managers—24 percent—say they have fired an employee for being dishonest. Clearly this is a growing problem that we must face head-on.

Honesty in the workplace creates energy, creativity, and productivity. Any of us who own or manage companies know what a treasure it is to have staff who live in the light of honesty. They bring life and energy into a company and become a beacon for other employees.

It is time to create new methods of developing greater honesty in our companies. Honesty and truth begin with leadership. Leaders must work together to reward, encourage, model, and display honesty at every level of a company's structure.

Simple practices are an easy way to begin. At staff meetings make sure all comments and ideas are received with respect and dignity. This makes everyone feel his or her input is valued and opens the atmosphere for more honesty. Make sure each manager has regular meetings with all staff members to tell them they are valued and that the managers deeply listen to their employees' concerns and ideas.

Laughter and balance in the workplace foster happiness, which leads to more openness and honesty. Play is a part of our human nature, and when we exhibit playfulness, the work atmosphere relaxes and allows everyone to be his or her true self at work. Leaders displaying vulnerability at work give others courage to tell the truth about who they are and what they value.

You may begin to bring more honesty and truth into your workplace in your own workspace. Display photos of your family, favorite pets, or great vacations. This tells those you work with what you love and who you are. Put your favorite inspirational quotes in a simple frame on your desk or wall. Visible truths that inspire and motivate you will keep you honest about who you are and what is important to you. It also inspires others in your office and gives them insight into the true you.

Keep your favorite colors and fabrics around you at work. If you love orange, make sure you have a shawl, picture frame, chair, or wall painted with your favorite color. Surrounding ourselves and others with our favorite colors and meaningful mementos are methods of honesty in our workplace.

As we begin to open up to others in our workplace, we share with others our intimate self. When one person is honest, others will join the flow, and the workplaces will function with more grace, ease, determination, and humility.

BEGIN TODAY

What is my excuse for not being honest at work?

Ask *Your Self*

What can I do today to be honest at work?

Tell *Your Self*

I am my true, honest, wonderful self at work.

Give *Your Self*

Create your workspace to reflect your true self.

CHAPTER **13**

Honesty with My Community

AWARE OF THE SUFFERING CAUSED BY LIES, DECEIT, AND DISHONESTY, I AM COMMITTED TO HONESTY WITH MY COMMUNITY.

Years ago, when my daughter was a senior in high school, I received a phone call mid-afternoon from the Atlanta police department. They asked me to come over to the home of my daughter's best friend. They did not give me details but asked me to come immediately. I knew the girl's mother, Susan, so I knew the way to her home, and when I got there the entire street was lined with police cars, an ambulance, and a coroner's car. I took a deep breath and slowly walked up to the house.

In the driveway was Susan's car with a tarp over the driver's side window. A very kind-faced police officer met me at the door, and after I identified myself he walked me into the house. There on the table was a suicide note that he handed me. I read it in horror, tears, and disbelief. Susan had left a suicide note asking me to care for her daughter. Then she walked out to her car, sat in the driver's seat, and put a gun to her head and killed herself.

I had just sat beside her the day before at our daughters' basketball game. We cheered and laughed and talked about where our girls were headed to college. What did I miss? I am a trained counselor, and I missed it. I felt responsible. Why couldn't she have told me her plans?

Maybe it wasn't planned. Maybe something happened that day that put her over the edge. But there was something incredible in that suicide note. She told us she was joining her mother, who had also committed suicide many years before. This massive, destructive secret was kept in the silence of her mind. Her mother suffered from profound psychological problems that also had plagued Susan in her silence. That secret may have led her to the same awful demise. How many of us have opened a newspaper or turned on the television and experienced shock and disbelief when we discovered a prominent member of our community or a neighbor had committed suicide? The conversation around the dinner table always goes, "I couldn't believe Darin Jones shot himself yesterday. I just saw him at the drug store last week, and he was his nice, smiling self. He was a deacon at the church and a pillar of the community. What in the world could have happened to him? There must have been something going on."

Whenever this happened to me growing up, I would wonder, What were the secrets in that house? Did we see what we wanted to see? Did Darin act differently recently, but we were all too busy to notice? Did he call out for help in some way that no one noticed? Why didn't any of us in the community notice?

Why do we keep a happy face in our communities? Why do we perform for others? Why do we show up at social functions and no matter how many people come up to us and ask, "How are you?" we answer in rote cadence, "Oh, I am fine." The social attendees continue: "Anything new?" "No, nothing really." Most of us show up at social functions as zombies or on display, wanting to look like Barbie or Ken dolls, in fear of gossip or not being invited to the next event.

Why do we continue to stay in community organizations that do not serve our truth? Why do we serve in organizations that are dead and do not give us meaning in our lives?

Every moment of our lives is sacred and is to be lived in our own truth. Participating in an organization that creates truth and meaning in your life will give you life. Research shows that people who belong to a group that gives them meaning live longer and experience greater health.

When you sit on a board or belong to an organization, tell the truth! When you meet and they ask your opinion, be honest. Don't join up to be accepted and begin to agree with people you don't agree with just to be accepted. This world needs your truth. We need more honesty in our world.

Every organization needs each of us to stand up with honesty. When you are honest, you are powerful and transform others' lives.

I have been blessed to sit on many boards in my life. Most of the boards I have served work with the impoverished and groups in need. I always felt that the greatest gift I could contribute was honesty.

I sat on a board in the inner city of Atlanta in one of the most at-risk, dangerous housing areas in the country. Our organization supported this inner-city community with after-school programs, tutoring, a library, and many wonderful programs to help their children and families.

At my first meeting, when they asked me what I would like to do on the board, I answered, "Just tell me the job no one wants to do." They laughed and pointed out the window to a group of young kids on the playground who should have been in school. They were a tough group, and no one wanted to get near them. I told the board I wanted to work with the "throw-away kids" on that playground. I walked out and sat listening to those amazing little souls for over an hour. I promised to work with them if they promised to stay in school. Most of those children ended up finishing high school and have gone on to either higher education or great jobs.

Fresh eyes on a board see with a keen sense of honesty what others may not have seen or have glossed over. It is our job, our responsibility to be fiercely honest when we sit on boards as leaders and serve others. We are required to challenge, question, and demand answers of honesty. Some people sitting on boards are always creating problems. Be honest with the chair, and discuss methods of dealing with the antagonistic person.

Our world is crying out for an era of honesty in all aspects of our life. You are being called to be in this wave of new, innovative leadership in our global family by being the symbol of the power and courage of honesty. Honesty is brave. Each time we move beyond our egos of what we want people to think and tell them the truth, we become part of something bigger.

BEGIN TODAY

What is my excuse for not being honest in my community?

Ask *Your Self*

How can I be more honest in my community?

Tell *Your Self*

I have the courage to be honest at all times.

Give *Your Self*

Speak your truth in your community.

CHAPTER 14

Optimism: The Second Commitment

Every Obstacle Is an Opportunity

> **AWARE OF THE SUFFERING CAUSED BY PESSIMISM, NEGATIVITY, AND HOPELESSNESS, I AM COMMITTED TO PRACTICING OPTIMISM IN EVERY FACET OF MY LIFE.**

Newly released scientific studies confirm the health benefits of a "Pollyanna" attitude. Research shows optimistic individuals enjoy a host of health benefits such as a reduced risk of cardiovascular disease, hypertension, and infections. A recent study reveals that optimistic individuals reduced their risk of death by 50 percent over the nine years of the study.

Maintaining a positive outlook on life has direct benefits on aging. This doesn't surprise me after working with a cardiac rehabilitation group for years. In my experience most of the geriatric patients who have survived painful life events are optimistic. In addition, those patients had a great effect upon the patients who were pessimistic or "sour." The more positive patients brightened the rooms they were in, generating energy.

Gail was one of my pulmonary patients and had chronic bronchitis and emphysema. She wore her small oxygen tank on her back, papoose oxygen, every day of her life. She struggled to breathe, and most of her life she was tethered on a leash by her oxygen cord when she wasn't wearing it on her back. Still, she was full of optimism and joy. Purple was her favorite color, and she would parade around in her lavender garb like a queen.

Gail was an inspiration to all of us when we would have bad days because we got a bill in the mail or we didn't make as much money as we wanted. She kept her eye on the prize with optimism. She focused on the sun shining or how lucky she was to have our group or a phone call from a friend. She treasured the simple, ordinary, and mundane things in life as if they were gifts from heaven above.

When I received a call from the hospital that she was dying and wanted me there, I raced through my house to find anything I had that was purple. In her hospital room, she was smiling even while gasping for air. After I kissed her, I gently placed a rich purple shawl over her white hospital blanket, hung a purple painting on the wall, put purple amethyst beads in her hand, and put purple booties on her fragile, cold feet. We both laughed, and the room full of her friends and family couldn't keep the tears back. Gail was in purple heaven. The next day her doctor called to ask me what I had done to Gail. She told me Gail was walking up and down the hospital halls drenched in her purple garb and was miraculously better. Gail lived almost a year after her jolt of purple optimism. Gail was one of many patients who were inspirations to me by living lives rooted in optimism.

Optimism is a tendency to expect the best possible outcome. Optimists believe that the universe is always evolving toward good, that good triumphs over evil, and that people are inherently good. The traditional definition of an optimist is that you see the glass as half full instead of half empty. Pessimists see their role as diminished, insignificant, their lack of action shrinking the big picture to a pinhole. Optimists see the "bigger picture" and themselves as having a significant or meaningful role.

I come from a gene pool of eternal optimists. My father was a salesman and lived each day whistling as he headed out the door expecting that to be the week he had the most sales in his career. At night after his sales job during the day, my father drove a dump truck from northern Ohio to the coal mines in southern Ohio to get coal to earn more money for our family. He would let me ride with him some nights. It was a special treat, because I would stay up all night despite having school the next day. There was no heat in the truck, and he would do this even in the dead of winter. These were some of the few times I had a "good time" with my father, so I remember those trips well. Unlike so many of his tyrannical evenings of darkness with our family, he was joyous when he was working and telling stories.

During those long, cold nights my father would talk about the difficult sales he had made and how exciting it was to be a salesman. He was not just hopeful, but optimistic, that every sale would eventually transpire. He always said you have to believe in yourself, your product, and the public. This incredibly powerful energy would emanate from him as he would talk about how life was all about being positive about the outcome.

My mother was devoutly religious, and she believed that the power of God would overcome anything, anywhere, at any time. No matter how bad a situation or a particular person was in my mind, she would find a silver lining in any dark cloud. My optimism was born out of an interesting combination of parents. When we would complain about a mean teacher at dinner, my mother would remind us that teachers have so much responsibility on their shoulders and are called by God to teach, so we should pray for them.

Researchers are verifying what my parents, aunts, uncles, and grandparents taught me many years ago. My granddaddy made breakfast every morning of his life while singing happy songs in the kitchen. I would run to the kitchen to be closer to all that oozing optimism. Aunt Pat, who was a nurse, would clean up my scraped knee after a bicycle accident and say, "This is a kiss from an angel so you will remember her."

We know through research that every thought or emotion we experience has electrical energy and a chemical response attached to it. Therefore, when you are optimistic you are sending healing hormones all over your body that boost your immune system and create health in your mind, body, and soul. The *Journal of Personality and Psychology* released a study that found people who had positive attitudes toward aging lived an average of seven and a half years longer than those who viewed aging in a negative manner.

Margery Silver of the New England Centenarian study at Beth Deaconess Medical Center studied the psychological profiles of two hundred healthy centenarians. She discovered the common theme that runs through these centenarians is that they remain positive thinkers. A study in the *Archives of General Psychiatry* showed after ten years of follow-up, people who were very optimistic had a 55 percent lower risk of death from all causes and a 23 percent lower risk of heart-related death, compared with people who reported a high level of pessimism. The MacArthur Foundation Study of Aging in America showed that lifestyle choices are more important than genetics in determining the quality of an individual's aging.

Optimists laugh more, and laughter creates health and well-being. A study at the University of Maryland Medical Center shows laughter

hold my suffering at bay for a little while, but then it would emerge in the most fragile times of my life and devastate me. The more I attempted to rid myself of my suffering, the more I felt like a failure when it returned and grew.

The Buddhists deal with the problem of suffering better than any other religious or self-help program I had tried before. The Second Noble Truth—suffering is caused by our cravings and attachments—was a difficult concept for me at first. It took many teachers and lots of learning and practice to realize I was attached to my suffering in some perverse way. I held on to it like a badge of courage. It was an identity from which I could not free myself. I craved love and acceptance by everyone; my suffering was caused by my cravings and attachments.

Talk about a lightbulb moment. I loved my husband and two daughters tremendously. I was obsessed with making them happy so they would love me more and therefore would never leave me. What an exhausting, fear-based way to live. I wanted to be popular and for others to love me, so I spent much of my life worried about the right clothes, furniture, homes, cars, education, weight, and hair color. How sad my life was. The Buddhists were perfectly correct. I was attached to everything, and my cravings for status, wealth, health, and love were insatiable. But the truth is so liberating.

I longed for the knowledge of how to experience freedom from my suffering. I discovered this in the Third Noble Truth by learning detachment methods. The more I meditated, the more I witnessed my anger or fear popping up in interesting ways. The more I meditated, the more I realized how much space my accumulation of all my life's suffering took up in my life, leaving little room for true joy and happiness.

The Fourth Noble Truth promised freedom from suffering through the Eightfold Path, which includes these elements:

1. **Right view (wisdom)**

2. **Right intention (positive mental energy that controls our actions)**

3. **Right speech (words that heal)**

4. **Right action (our good deeds)**

5. **Right livelihood (earn our living in a moral way)**

6. **Right effort (wholesome mental energy)**

7. **Right mindfulness (clear perception)**

8. **Right concentration (practice of meditation)**

I had spent an enormous amount of time and a massive amount of energy trying to push away suffering, trying to mask the pain, trying to keep busy working so I couldn't feel the pain. What I learned from Wong Loh Sin See, Thich Nhat Hanh, and His Holiness the Dalai Lama is that we all suffer. Suffering is the human condition, so I need not judge myself as bad or defective because of this suffering. It is universal, and there is a tried, tested, and proven path for over two thousand years that will lead you through it. It was such a relief to me that I didn't have to try to kill it, force it away, or go to one more healer to extract the pain. All I had to do was sit with it and allow it to emerge, detach from the pain, view it, and grace my suffering with compassion.

People often ask how I can rescue dogs with problem behaviors, injuries, or trauma from abuse. I welcome these damaged dogs, as I have my suffering patients, to Oak Haven. Here we all have the space and permission to discover our source of suffering. We sit with it, explore the wound, and transform this suffering into joy. I have learned over many years that I don't "fix" anything. I offer a path to healing and act as a witness. As we move past each obstacle of suffering, we have the ability to gain wisdom and grow spiritually and emotionally. Every obstacle in our lives is truly an opportunity for growth.

As I have continued in this path, I have grown more courageous and confident, because I have experienced obstacles that open doors to a life of joy and abundance.

It may feel counterintuitive to accept suffering in order to live optimistically, but it works. Accepting something dilutes its power to dominate our thoughts and our lives, making room for clarity and peace. Adopting a Buddhist approach to my suffering was part of beginning to experience obstacles as opportunities, which leads to optimism.

When that began to happen, I left the river I had been traveling, searching for what felt like home. I settled at Oak Haven by the spring that created Lake Sautee. I had found my watering hole, where I could be filled up with optimism. Every day, living in the cycles of nature and seasons infused me with a new optimism. My life was no longer a daily battle against obstacles, but a limitless choice of opportunities to be optimistic. I learned to embrace obstacles, knowing within each one is planted a seed of opportunity.

In the next chapters we will explore specific ways to learn how to live a life of optimism. You will discover how to become optimistic in your own life, in your relationship with the Divine, with your partner, in your family, at work, and in your community.

CHAPTER 15

Optimism with My Self

AWARE OF THE SUFFERING CAUSED BY PESSIMISM, NEGATIVITY, AND HOPELESSNESS, I AM COMMITTED TO PRACTICING OPTIMISM WITH MY SELF.

The snow was blowing so hard I couldn't see outside the Student Aid office at Ohio State University. I tried to hide the embarrassment of my tattered brown coat, rolling under the frayed sleeves. I was nineteen years old, and all I owned in the world were the clothes in a plastic bag sitting next to me. After I got my student loan and work study forms stamped "Approved," I had to face the fact I had nowhere to stay, nothing to eat, and only twenty-two dollars in my purse. I was so focused on getting into college, I figured I'd handle the details of a roof over my head and food at some later time.

Through the grace of God I managed to contact a friend from childhood who had ended up at OSU. David kindly allowed me to live in the basement of the house where he lived with his roommates if I would clean and cook.

I had made a promise to myself that I would get an education so I would never end up like my mother, who was dependent on my father for everything. I made weekly calls to my mother to make sure she was safe from my father's rage. One night my normal weekly call turned into a 911 event. My father had threatened to kill my mother again, had taken the keys to the cars, and was keeping her captive in their home. I had an ancient Volkswagen Bug with no floorboards and bald tires. I had no money for gas to rescue her or any money for anything, for that matter.

That night as I was washing the dishes after my classes at Ohio State, my tears dripped into the dishwater. The guys had the national evening news on very loud in the next room when I heard, "I'm Jimmy Carter, and as your governor of Georgia I want to help our citizens in need. I lived a simple life in Plains, Georgia, and I have experienced people in difficult times, and I want to help these Georgians." Governor Carter was on national television talking about his passion for those impoverished in Georgia. I rushed over to see him as he continued to speak on the television, and thought instantly, *He can help me.*

As I gazed out to the mounting snow outside, I wrote the kind governor from Georgia a letter that night and pleaded my case. I told him I was a hard worker and would do anything if he could help me get some money or find a way to help my mom, who was one of those Georgians "in need." I was brutally honest and asked him to help me so my dad wouldn't kill my mom. As I licked the envelope, I felt a fierce sense of courage and dignity. I knew this man would help me.

The governor of Georgia wrote me back. Days later my heart was beating out of my chest as I ripped open the letter.

Dear Ms. Hall,

I am sorry to hear about these terrible circumstances in your life. Rest assured, I am going to assist you so you can get to your mother. I have secured a job for you in Columbus, Georgia, and have secured a place for you at Columbus College. Please contact me to tell me exactly what you need to get here, and when you arrive you will have income and a school to attend.

Sincerely,

Jimmy Carter

Governor Carter fed my hope and optimism by listening to my honest, heartfelt plea for help. He used his power to turn my obstacles into opportunities for me to help my family and my future.

MENTORS OF OPTIMISM

The greatest leaders in every field are optimists. Think of your greatest teacher. Visualize her or him in your mind right now. Recall the voice that spoke to you. Now remember the spiritual leader in your life that had the greatest effect upon you. This minister, priest, rabbi, imam, guru, or nun inspired you to think differently about yourself and to perhaps have a vision for your future. Remember how powerful these images are and how they transformed your life.

When I was attending Emory University for one of my graduate degrees, I met world leaders whose greatness was coupled with immense optimism.

Bishop Desmond Tutu's challenge of apartheid was a David and Goliath story for modern times. I was privileged to have classes with him at Emory when he taught there on sabbatical. He told intense stories of literally looking death in the face and of surviving extreme suffering. After these rich, long narrations he always asked if the students had any questions. The perennial question from the students was "Bishop Tutu, how did you fight this oppression, death, slaughter, and horror for so many years, and suffer so much, and not want to fight or retaliate?" He would listen tenderly and answer softly with words to this effect: "Most of these oppressed people who had survived unheard of horrors for many years wanted to retaliate, wanted to quit their passive stance and start fighting back. I knew the power I had, and therefore it was my responsibility to always be the beacon of optimism and hope for the future. Hope and optimism are a palpable energy driven by God and justice. I know the light and love of optimism and hope will always overcome the darkness. It just may not be on our timetable."

His Holiness the Dalai Lama was also teaching on campus while I was at Emory. The Dalai Lama had witnessed the slaughter of his monks in Tibet and was driven into exile by the Chinese Communists. He could have lived a quiet, peaceful life in exile in India, and the world would have gone on without ever really knowing about the country of Tibet. But the Dalai Lama knew the world needed to hear his Buddhist message of compassion and love for all beings.

If you have been in his presence you never forget his infectious smile and heavenly laughter. The cadence of his voice and the gentleness of his words continue to inspire millions around the globe. He could have accepted his exile in shame, anger, and silence, but he chose hope and optimism.

I took classes with President Jimmy Carter as well. Although President Carter lost his reelection bid, he did not lose his vision for this planet. He made a commitment to witness free elections in all nations. He decided to eradicate the horrendous guinea worm disease from Africa. He chose to be a voice for peace and nonviolence in the world, and the Carter Center became a point of light for humanitarianism and peace around the globe. He embodies the words "Every obstacle is an opportunity."

What can just one optimist do? Go to Africa and ask the millions who suffered the plague of painful guinea worms growing inside their bodies. The guinea worm is almost nonexistent in Africa today because of the efforts of President Jimmy Carter, one optimistic man. Each of these astonishing lives is an inspiration to accomplish our own dreams and visions despite obstacles.

THE SCIENCE OF OPTIMISM

Science tells us that optimism is actually a component of our DNA. You can look back to your ancestors and see the imprints of optimism. About half of your optimism comes from your DNA and half comes from your environment. But if you weren't born with optimistic DNA or didn't receive doses of it in your environment as you were growing up, it is not too late. You can learn how to become optimistic.

Why should you become optimistic?

- **First, you will have a richer life and have more fun.**

- **Second, you will attract happier people around you for a more supportive life.**

- **Third, your family will reap the benefits of your optimism.**

- **Fourth, you will live a healthier life and live longer if you are optimistic.**

One of the first steps to creating greater optimism in your life is to say a positive affirmation each time you feel like complaining or saying "Why me?" I usually say, "Good will come out of this." I may not see it at the time of crisis or in the middle of the obstacle, but everything happens for a reason, and as dark as this situation is, there is a purpose for it, and I trust the situation. I believe this is the greatest gift of this philosophy and commitment.

The world is full of people who say, "That's just my luck" or "This always happens to me." Life is one letdown after another in their perspective. You experience a life of joy and incredible happiness when you really believe that everything happens for a purpose and every obstacle really is an opportunity.

Another strategy to practice is when difficult obstacles occur, and they will, you learn to observe the situation; don't react immediately. You trust the situation and begin to view your life with more acceptance, wisdom, and grace instead of stress, fear, and reactivity. When you believe that you are part of a great Divine plan, and that every obstacle is there to cultivate your progress toward love, you develop a wonderful confidence and peace about your life.

Explore optimistic people you admire throughout history or in the current public realm. But don't forget you can be inspired by someone at your office, your neighbor, or the person at your dry cleaner. Some of the greatest optimists in my life were discovered in places like horse barns, grocery stores, or my car repair shop. Listen deeply to the way they live, ask them questions, and don't forget to thank them for inspiring your life.

Read books by inspirational and motivational people that you enjoy. They will water your soul with optimism. We are all thirsty for this kind of positive encouragement. Negative thoughts and messages to your self create conditions similar to stagnating water, where the only things that thrive are pesky mosquitoes. Positive thoughts and affirmations stir the spirit and create energy to move along new paths toward freedom to be who you were meant to be.

BEGIN TODAY

What is my excuse for not living optimistically?

Ask *Your Self*

What ways can I create more optimism in my life?

Tell *Your Self*

Every obstacle is an opportunity.

Give *Your Self*

Read a book about a person whose life has inspired you.

CHAPTER 16

Optimism with the Divine

AWARE OF THE SUFFERING CAUSED BY PESSIMISM, NEGATIVITY, AND HOPELESSNESS, I AM COMMITTED TO PRACTICING OPTIMISM WITH THE DIVINE.

There is an old adage that says, "If God is for you, then who can be against you?" Sadly, not everyone may want you to find happiness and peace with the Divine. It might cramp their style.

Alan was a patient who came to me after his diagnosis of advanced prostate cancer to figure out what to do with the rest of his life. Quite the pessimist and agnostic, suspicious of everyone and everything, Alan had lived a very cautious life for sixty-five years. He had inherited great wealth but had also worked hard in his very successful financial empire. He was admittedly a control freak.

Alan had never been spiritual or religious. He always thought someday spirituality would seep into his life as naturally as his gray hair, age spots, and receding hairline had done. In a flash this rotten cancer told him to "wake up." He was waking up to the idea that it was his responsibility and choice to pursue a spiritual life just as he had intentionally chosen to pursue a successful and busy business life. He was terrified as he realized he was racing against time as this cancer was ravaging his body.

He was raised a Southern Baptist and had rejected the hellfire and brimstone of his childhood a long time ago. He felt all religions were the same and designed for the weak. So Alan and I started out on a grand odyssey to learn about what different religions and spiritualities believed about the Divine and what part humans played in the design of the universe.

Alan also wanted to learn spiritual practices like meditation and yoga. I taught him meditation, and he learned a few yoga poses that gave him comfort and peace. Alan read spiritual books by a variety of universal voices as he sat alone and weak in the toasty grand sunroom of his privileged compound. We became very close during his final journey on this earth.

There were some surprising obstacles in his last months. His wife called me one day and asked me to meet her at her private country club for lunch the next day. (She belonged to the kind of country club for which you have to have genealogy papers to verify your lineage to become a member.)

As I walked into the club I saw Alan's wife, Lillian, and their son, Peter, sitting at a table with a perfectly starched white linen tablecloth topped by tiny lavender orchids. As I walked in everyone politely stood up. Lillian informed me that she had already ordered the chef's luncheon special for all of us. She showed me that my iced tea was awaiting me with a sprig of mint bent over the crystal goblet.

"Thank you for coming on such short notice. Peter and I had hoped we would not need to have this meeting, but we had no choice. Alan was diagnosed about one year ago, and they gave him a few months to live. Our family had made peace with his imminent death. He was sent to you for you to help him die peacefully. This has not turned out as we expected. He has lived for almost a year now. He is acting like a crazy hippie. We don't like what you are doing with him, and we want you to stop immediately."

I was dumbfounded, shocked, and enraged. After I gathered myself and took a sip of iced tea and a very deep breath, I said, "But Alan is so happy. He has been on a spiritual adventure for the last year like a kid in a candy store. He is one of the kindest, most tender people I have ever known. He is not the same man who walked into my office dying of cancer."

"Precisely, Dr. Hall. Dad was dying and I had taken over the company, and we expected for him to stay on the back sunporch, grow his orchids, and peacefully die within the short time frame the doctors gave us," said Peter.

"Sorry to disappoint both of you," I responded, trying not to sneer, "but Alan has found the real Alan, and he is experiencing joy. I wonder why Alan's lifestyle changes bother you so much. All he is doing is meditating on his cushion, eating a vegetarian diet, going to yoga class, and reading and talking about new and different things."

"Exactly," Lillian hissed. "Our friends at the club and our family think he has gone stark-raving mad. I am embarrassed for our friends and family to see him and talk to him. The last time friends came over he was barefoot, and I thought I would die. We want this bizarre behavior to stop immediately. Your services are no longer needed."

As I stood to leave I said, "We will see what Alan has to say about that." I called Alan several times over the next two days, and he didn't call back. I was concerned. So after work I drove by his home and saw the light in the sunroom on. I walked up and knocked on the glass door. He looked up from his book and motioned me into the room.

"Are you OK?" I hugged him and sat on the couch beside him. He shrugged his shoulders and tears began to cascade down his thin white cheeks. I saw the tissue box and handed him a tissue and held his hand. "What's going on?"

"I can't do this anymore," Alan said. "My family is really frustrated with me, and I am making them unhappy. Lillian told me to choose her or my new life with this new God. I love what I have discovered in this short time. I am not afraid to die. I now know this Holy One is quite the optimist. Every religion I studied showed me God believed in me with every breath I took. This cancer has been a real struggle for me, as you well know. But I never would have met you or found myself or believed in an afterlife of some kind if I didn't have this damn disease.

"I am going to do as Lillian and Peter have asked, Kathleen. No more of my embarrassing them. No more vegetarian diet. I'll stop my yoga and stop ordering my books on world spiritualities. I will always be grateful to you, but I am done." He stood up, held my hand, walked me to the door, and kissed me on the cheek, and I walked crying to my car.

Two weeks later I received a phone call from one of Alan's friends telling me Alan had died that morning. He said Lillian found him in his bed, and he had the prayer beads I had given him in his hand and the statue of St. Francis I had brought back for him from Assisi on the table by the bed. She said he had a faint smile on his face and the room felt very peaceful.

Alan taught me many valuable lessons. The first is that people always have the power of choice over their own lives and that we should not take their choices personally. Alan had a right to say he was done for whatever reasons he had. I also learned about the tremendous power of families. The desire to be loved and accepted overpowered the will to live. Alan taught me detachment and surrender.

Every religion in the world portrays the Divine as optimistic. God is *the* optimist. If we go back to our childhoods, many of us grew up with a notion that God was always watching over us and wanted the best for us. When we did bad things, we knew God would forgive us and love us if we confessed and tried to do a little better.

Whether we are depressed, angry, rejected, or fearful, we know that there is an energy, a force, that many of us call God, driving us forward to a better place. The Bible and all great religious scriptures are filled with stories of wayward individuals who get back on track with the help of this optimistic God. You may read inspirational or religious books, join spiritual or religious groups, seek advice from a cleric or holy person, or take a class that interests you. There are many things you can do to remain optimistic about the Divine in the face of difficulties.

Nature is a perennial source of Divine optimism. Every spectrum of nature fosters the seeds of Divine optimism. Each of the four seasons beckons us to the next phase of our lives. The mystical phases of the moon lure us into optimism and wonder. The powerful forces of nature beam the energy of optimism to us through each ray of summer sunlight, the refreshing sweet smells of the cool fall air, the winter winds summoning spring, and the single droplets of spring rain exciting us with expectations of summer. Nature is the womb of Divine optimism.

I taught world religions, and it was wonderful to see how similar all great religions experience the Divine. Whether it is the Bible, the Talmud, the Koran, the Upanishads, the Vedas, the I Ch'ing, or the Discourses of Buddha, the Divine is the wind blowing through us and behind us, urging us on to a better life.

As I grew, I realized that my parents were mired in the tragic struggle of their own lives. The one constant source of peace, power, and optimism was my immersion in the Divine. No matter how difficult life got, and believe me, there were many treacherous times, I knew that there was this Holy Essence that created me and wanted something greater. This is the optimistic Spirit that propels the universe and is the driver in all creation.

Survival itself is one optimistic event after another. A dog with puppies nurses them trusting that each has what it needs to survive and thrive. Every species on the planet trusts the process with incredible optimism. You don't see many creatures, other than humans, worrying and planning for the worst—or complaining when things are going well.

No matter where you are now in your life, that optimistic Divine being is cheering for you, loving you, guiding you, and sending you hope. You may not see the hope right now, but look around you. We discover hope in the most humble places: the sun on your face, a breeze through your hair, your dog wagging her tail as she rubs against you, the smile of a person passing you in the mall, or a cool glass of water when you are thirsty. The well is never empty when you turn to the Divine. Don't ever give up on the Divine; she isn't giving up on you!

BEGIN TODAY

What is my excuse for not believing in an optimistic Divine spirit?

Ask *Your Self*

Is optimism one of the characteristics of the Divine I experience?

Tell *Your Self*

In everything give thanks, for it is a gift from the Divine.

Give *Your Self*

Visit a local botanical garden or wildlife preserve and experience Divine optimism in nature.

CHAPTER 17

Optimism with My Partner

AWARE OF THE SUFFERING CAUSED BY PESSIMISM, NEGATIVITY, AND HOPELESSNESS, I AM COMMITTED TO PRACTICING OPTIMISM WITH MY PARTNER.

I have been married to the same man for a very long time. My husband's parents were married for more than fifty years, so Jim's experience of marriage was one of stability, love, and respect. My parents were divorced after a twenty-three-year destructive marriage—their marriage was like moving from one roller coaster ride to another: dangerous, up and down, upside down, and a true nightmare. We could not have had more diverse experiences.

Jim has always been the optimist in our marriage. He is the one who encourages me and has had rock-solid confidence in each stage of our relationship. Jim is tender, kind, selfless, a great father, a "Mr. Mom." He is a very busy physician who still insists on washing dishes, washing clothes, and vacuuming the floors.

I have been the partner who keeps waiting for the sky to fall in our marriage. I have been so damaged from my parents' marriage that after thirty-five years, in the back of my mind, I believe something terrible can still happen.

We have had the same problems all marriages have: money, sex, children, aging parents, and power issues. We have also been business partners for thirty-five years besides being married to each other. Hurricane, disaster, crisis, or collapse, my husband has the same two comments for every dilemma in our entire marriage: "It's all good" and "Never, ever, ever give up."

Jim continues to teach me optimism in marriage. We once came home from a two-day trip and opened the closet door to a foul smell. Our cat got locked in his closet while we were gone for the weekend. Fiona had urinated all over Jim's expensive Tumi luggage. It was ruined. He loves his Tumi luggage, so I held my breath as we looked at each other. He shrugged his shoulders and said, "It's all good. At least she didn't go on my new black shoes." Is that an optimist or what?

FOR BETTER OR WORSE

The institution of marriage is based on optimism. I believe the definition of marriage should include the word *optimism*. How can you stand before another person and repeat those vows and not have a seed of optimism within you? You pledge to stay with another person for the rest of your life through being rich or poor, sick or healthy. That's either optimistic or crazy!

Couples who commit to a partnership and move in together root their relationship in optimism. Both partners are giving up the security of their own homes and identities to forge a new committed relationship. This can be more challenging than a marriage, because there are not the legal guarantees married partners enjoy. Hope and optimism become the energy that drives these beautiful, rich relationships.

From the time we are young, many of us wonder if we will find someone to partner with for a lifetime. The moment we slip that ring on our finger the optimism begins careening downhill like a runaway vehicle. Before you know it, "optimism" creates a list of desires: a car, a home, a child, a new job, an education, and happiness.

You begin to build your life around this optimistic view of what you and your partner can have. This works for a while, but then reality enters the picture. Your partner doesn't make the amount of money you planned on; your credit report goes south along with your hopes for that new home. For some, plans for a child go off track when they face the painful dilemma of infertility and the choices and costs associated with this crisis in their marriage.

We start out our relationships with our lapel pin of optimism, but it can quickly get lost in the laundry. If one doesn't focus and create an intention of continued optimism in a relationship, it can evaporate, and as this occurs the fractures begin to take their toll. It is difficult, if not impossible, for only one partner to hold the optimism in a relationship. Optimism is a virtue that is best shared.

The first wound in a relationship usually involves finances. This is where fear, anxiety, anger, and depression can begin to plague two people in a committed partnership. The myth that two people can live as cheaply as one persists. That almost never happens. Whatever you do, don't wait until after you are married to begin talking honestly about money. Money can be a source of destruction or a source of creativity in a marriage. When, not if, money gets tight, think of it as an opportunity to see what you are made of individually and as a couple.

Don't let gloom and doom hook you. This may be an obstacle, but a great opportunity unfolds when you remember you have a partner to share in your financial journey. You have someone to grow with, learn with, and help shoulder financial challenges in your life. Think of your financial needs as an experiment. Or think of your money dilemma as a class you're taking called Money 101, and you are going to learn, as a couple, how you got here, what went wrong, and how to avoid this in the future.

I always suggest that each person in a relationship have some private money. Money is a source of power, and when one partner stays home or is not the primary wage earner, that person's self-esteem can suffer if he or she has no personal money or control over joint funds. If money becomes a problem when you are arguing, please seek help immediately. There are counselors who are fabulous and can help you create a healthier partnership, especially around the issues of money.

Sex is another area where your relationship can be wounded if you are together long enough. Try to be optimistic about your sex life. It will wane and wax and be different during the stages of a long marriage, but please always be optimistic. Remember, you are in this relationship for a lifetime. Each of you changes over your life, and this means sex will be one of the first places you will notice something is not right. Please set a time once a week, over coffee or dinner, to talk about how each of you feels in regard to your sex life. When I did counseling, so many people had let their sex life slip away. The fact is, if you are not having sex with your partner, one or both of you eventually will be having sex with someone else. The only thing more painful than an affair is if your spouse leaves you for another person.

When problems happen, go to a relationship counselor or a sex therapist. My husband and I have been to both, and they have transformed our lives into something new and better than before. Don't be afraid or embarrassed to go. The individuals who do this counseling are wonderfully trained. It is like going to school and learning about a new perspective that is fun and life-giving. Most importantly, keep optimistic about sex.

When you go out on your weekly dates as a couple, talk about the science of optimism and discuss how you can learn to be more optimistic with each other. Check in with each other regularly and do an optimism checkup on your relationship. Are you the cheerleader for your partner?

It's not only fun to be in an optimistic relationship, but you also set an example for others. An optimistic partnership is a gift to your children, your community, and our world. Relationships are subject to tides and currents. That must be accepted. Occasionally the creek runs dry. But if you address the problems early, you can create new energy and channels to keep the relationship fluid.

BEGIN TODAY

What is my excuse for not being an optimist with my partner?

Ask *Your Self*

What can I do to learn to be optimistic in my relationship?

Tell *Your Self*

I believe every obstacle in my relationship is an opportunity for a better relationship.

Give *Your Self*

As a couple, go to a counselor for an optimism checkup.

CHAPTER 18

Optimism with My Family

> **AWARE OF THE SUFFERING CAUSED BY PESSIMISM, NEGATIVITY, AND HOPELESSNESS, I AM COMMITTED TO PRACTICING OPTIMISM WITH MY FAMILY.**

Ryan was sitting in a jail cell waiting for his trial for driving under the influence. Ryan is an eighteen-year-old, good-looking, smart young man from a nice middle-class family. His mother is a hardworking teacher, his father owns a large company, and his younger brother is in school. Ryan was a great student who had never had a day of trouble until he made friends with a new boy at school who drank alcohol and smoked marijuana. It wasn't long before Ryan gave in to peer pressure in order to fit in with his new friend's group.

In the last year Ryan had been picked up twice for drinking while driving; the third time he was locked up. His parents were so furious they felt unable to communicate with Ryan. Ryan and his parents argued so bitterly that their family situation had escalated to the point of crisis. They were referred to a friend of mine who gave them some good advice.

Ryan's parents had been treating him like a loser criminal with no hope for a future. Ryan felt such shame and self-loathing that he had stopped attempting to relate to his parents. He said he knew no one believed in him, so he wondered why he should even try to communicate. His parents had no idea how their disapproval, judgment, and shaming had helped cause Ryan's alienation. They thought they were doing their job by being clear that his behavior was unacceptable.

The therapist encouraged the family to be optimistic with Ryan. This was not a life sentence for him, but an obstacle in his life that had created the opportunity to bring his family together and move them to a different level of love and communication. The family had to learn that each family member was going to encounter many obstacles in their lives. It was the job of each person in the family to support one another, be a source of inspiration and optimism, through each learning experience. They began weekly family meetings where each person talked about the stresses in their lives and asked for help from other family members in times of need. They learned how to create healthy boundaries in one another's lives. They also learned effective tools through Al-Anon to deal with an addicted family member.

Ryan is a sophomore at a local college now and has a job and a dog. He plays first base on the baseball team, and his family comes to watch him play each week. They have family meetings at a pizza joint after his games. Ryan's problem with drinking and driving turned out to be not an insurmountable obstacle, but a bump in the road of life.

Because the family chose to jump in and learn how to look at things differently, they were able to heal the damage to their family. When they understood that Ryan was looking for ways to be accepted and for approval rather than just rebelling against their standards and expectations, they were able to share their faith with Ryan. Although he had to suffer consequences for his actions, they were still his family and believed he could move beyond his past and into a better future.

THE ROOTS OF OPTIMISM

Optimism in a family is rooted in the parents. The parents set the stage on which the drama of family unfolds. If you think about any family right now you admire, the parents and siblings are cheerleaders for each other. You have to be able to convey that optimistic hope to one another in order to promote and preserve communication as children and adults grow and change.

Each person in the family system has different gifts and graces. The family has the opportunity to experience the gift of each person and organize itself so that it can support the dream of each family member. For example, the mother and father may have careers they love; one child is a great basketball player, and another child is a gifted violinist. The challenge of the family is to create the time and energy to support each member of the group. Families can get into trouble if they support the sports enthusiast by going to every Friday night game as a family event but overlook weeknight concerts by the violinist because they are inconvenient. Children innately know if you believe in them.

Because communication is essential, weekly family meetings are a must. You can think of your weekly family meeting as your pep rally. This is the time to share successes and failures in a safe environment. Successes are applauded, but no one boos at the failures. Instead they may listen with empathy and offer encouragement or strategies to overcome an obstacle.

Each week agree on a time for a thirty-minute family meeting. Attendance is mandatory, so everyone's schedule must be taken into consideration. A different person is the leader of the family meeting each week. This gives each person in the family the experience of power in the family. The meeting is started with a devotional given by the leader. This devotional can be on anything that the family member is interested in. For example, the basketball player may want to do a three-minute piece on Michael Jordan that she believes is inspirational.

The family can also have a concern and worry box they keep in a central place in the home. During the week family members write down what they are worried or concerned about at school, work, home, or with themselves and tuck it in the box to discuss at the meeting. Each week during the family meeting the leader opens the concern box and reads the concerns of the family members so that the entire family can give each person positive feedback, support, and encouragement. This is a critical practice for our busy, chaotic families.

Most of the problems and pain in families result from lack of communication that later moves into behavioral problems. Never underestimate how the power of optimism and encouragement fostered at these meetings can transform your family's life.

Optimism appears in many different forms. The neatness and decor of your home can create a happy, optimistic environment for the family to flourish in. When you visit a home that is dark, dirty, and messy, how do you feel? When you visit a home that is sunny, bright, and clean, how do you feel? We are nurtured by our senses, so the environment you choose for your family home is very important in fostering optimism.

If you are not much of a decorator, at least insist on cleanliness, and if you don't have time or are too tired to clean, give someone a chance to help. Either hire a housecleaner or trade someone for services. We each have skills that might benefit another person. Part of optimism is realizing you don't have to do everything yourself. Even a parent who has no interest in housekeeping or home decor can model creative solutions for their family.

Tough times will happen in a family. It may be a child failing a class, the emotional break up with a boyfriend, or the illness of a family member. The family is the safety net of optimism and hope that weaves these precious lives together. At these times optimistic family rituals can support and strengthen the family.

Our family always went out for ice cream. When a situation occurred in our family that was tough, we talked, walked, and went for ice cream. Maybe your family goes to a particular local restaurant, goes to the mall and a certain store, or rents a movie and eats popcorn. The family ritual is the glue of a family. My children are grown, and we still go for ice cream, eat at our favorite family restaurant, and watch *Steel Magnolias*. Optimism is grounded in family rituals. Please invest in your family by creating these intimate times that you will hold in your heart forever.

Holidays are occasions that instill optimism in a family. No matter what happens in a family during the years—deaths, divorces, arguments, or estrangements—holidays create the opportunity for hope, new beginnings, and healing. Don't allow holidays to become stale and rote. Weave new traditions into the fabric of your holiday rituals. Try new food, decorate with new colors, invite new people, or go to new places.

One of the purposes of family is to support all family members in developing their gifts and talents and achieving their goals. Your family is your advocate in life. They can be a source of optimism when the water rises, the wind whips up, and the whitecaps or rapids threaten to overturn the boat.

BEGIN TODAY

What is my excuse for not being more optimistic with my family?

Ask *Your Self*

How can we support each other more in our family?

Tell *Your Self*

Our family is the root of hope, optimism, and happiness.

Give *Your Self*

Once a week go out for a family dinner and enjoy laughter.

CHAPTER 19

Optimism with My Work

AWARE OF THE SUFFERING CAUSED BY PESSIMISM, NEGATIVITY, AND HOPELESSNESS, I AM COMMITTED TO PRACTICING OPTIMISM WITH MY WORK.

With climate change affecting the planet more and more every day, there are new, encouraging corporations starting up each day with phenomenal ideas for recycling our precious resources on this fragile planet.

One woman in Los Angeles found it troubling that millions of tires were filling up our landfills and felt there must be some recycling solution to this problem. Lindsay Smith then read that the city of Los Angeles was having massive problems with the roots of their beautiful old trees breaking up their cement sidewalks, and it was costing a fortune for the city to continue to repair the sidewalks. The problem grew to the point of considering cutting down these ancient trees to save the sidewalk repair costs.

This optimistic, creative woman invented a process where old tires were taken from landfills and recycled into sidewalk squares. These squares are laid on the ground, giving a pliable surface where the large roots can flourish underneath the soft sidewalks. When the roots grow larger, the tile is moved or replaced. The staggering costs for maintaining these sidewalks dropped to a minimal amount. More cities around the world are now using this optimistic solution to a great obstacle. Lindsay Smith turned two obstacles into an opportunity for a career.

Given the current economic crisis, optimistic leadership in our corporations is essential for a company to thrive and compete in our global economy. Every corporation must take the emerging brain science on optimism seriously. Just as you can infect a corporation with contagious stress, you can nurture a business environment with optimism.

Optimism can be a learned skill. Whether you are in a position of leadership or working with peers as a coworker, you can model behavior that teaches no matter what happens within your corporation or business setting, or in the global economy, every obstacle becomes an opportunity.

It is sad that the American automobile industry didn't learn this a long time ago. In the seventies, with the first gasoline shortages, we should have taken the lead in developing fuel-efficient, smaller cars. It is unbelievable that our American automobile makers continued to manufacture gas-guzzling, oversized SUVs. This obstacle in the seventies could have been an amazing opportunity for automakers, as it was for the Japanese. The Japanese automakers lived on a small island and knew firsthand about limited resources. They knew about the horrors of being dependent on other nations for oil. They chose to accept the challenge of change.

An extremely troublesome area of human relations management in the workplace is the tremendous increase in the levels of bullying and aggression. This makes it a challenge to create an optimistic work environment. Research tells us that positive, encouraging work environments are healthier, create less employee turnover, decrease absenteeism, and are more productive. Complaints of bullying must be taken seriously, as that kind of aggressive behavior will lower the morale of a workplace and affect productivity. Optimism cannot flourish where problems are not addressed.

Another common scenario is when one person in a work environment infects everyone with contagious stress. Contagious stress is a real phenomenon that has been studied in Europe for many years. Stress in a corporation can literally spread like a pandemic. For example, one person might spread rumors about layoffs because of cost cuts, and then fear spreads like wildfire through the company, setting off a panic. Studies have even located the places where these "stress viruses" originate, usually in restrooms or near a coffeepot.

We all know what it is like to go into work in a good mood and feel ourselves brought down or irritated by the office grump, gossip, or arrogant critic. This is no small factor within a corporation. Unchecked, it can wreak havoc with the optimism, productivity, and mood of a company.

You can initiate optimism at work by having an office lunch at least once a week. Either go out to a local restaurant or bring lunch and share your lives over a meal. You don't have to be Oprah to begin a book club that meets for thirty minutes once a week in the office break room. An office study group can create a deeper sense of trust, hope, and optimism in our companies. Your office surroundings can ground your company in optimism. Make sure your colors are bright and inspiring and there is lots of light in your offices. Research tells us music reduces stress and creates a sense of well-being. Play soothing, upbeat music at your office.

Design a community bulletin board where the staff can put up notes to list items they need or people who have goods they don't need can offer them to others. Someone may need baby furniture that another family has outgrown, and another person may have an extra computer they don't need anymore that someone else can use.

These initiatives can be fostered from the top down or bottom up. An infectious sense of hope, caring, and optimism springs from such acts for all to share and witness. We're in the same boat, and we all can lend a hand paddling.

BEGIN TODAY

What is my excuse for not being optimistic at work?

Ask *Your Self*

How can I build optimism at my workplace?

Tell *Your Self*

I am Ms./Mr. Optimism at work.

Give *Your Self*

Once a week eat with fellow coworkers.

CHAPTER 20

Optimism with My Community

AWARE OF THE SUFFERING CAUSED BY PESSIMISM, NEGATIVITY, AND HOPELESSNESS, I AM COMMITTED TO PRACTICING OPTIMISM WITH MY COMMUNITY.

"What if every child had a laptop?" That is the question Nicholas Negroponte asked after living in a remote village in Cambodia and returning to MIT as a professor. In Cambodia he witnessed how the lives of children and their families were positively impacted by their use of computers. As a result, Professor Negroponte decided that every child on the planet should have a computer. That was a huge dream, but optimism and passion provided the alchemy for his vision of a new world.

At MIT Negroponte amassed a group of geeks to attempt to create a one-hundred-dollar computer that was waterproof, dustproof, could hold a charge for at least ten hours, be Wi-Fi ready, and have a satellite connection. Only two years later his dream became a reality. The organization he inspired—One Laptop per Child—has distributed computers to the poorest countries in the world, from Uruguay, Haiti, and Mexico to Mongolia, Ghana, and the small Polynesian island of Niue, about 1.5 million kids so far. Not only are more children showing up for school, but when the kids take the laptops home, they teach the entire family how to use it.

Children around the globe now have access to more truth and knowledge via satellite. These children and families will have an opportunity to hear more than just government propaganda. Instead, they will have access to the news of current events and information from around the globe that is available on the Internet. Professor Nicholas Negroponte, one professor at MIT, turned an obstacle he saw into an opportunity. His optimism that education was an essential tool for solving world poverty led him to inspire others to use their creativity to help.

OUR FUTURE DEPENDS ON OPTIMISM

There has never been a time in human history when optimism in our local and world communities was more crucial for the survival of our planet. We have become isolated. Most of us are exhausted when we get home in the evening, and it takes all our energy to care for our family's needs. Our homes these days are designed with large back porches, but home design has done away with our front porches and our opportunity for true community.

For some, updating Facebook pages takes priority over face time with the people who live on our street or in our apartment building. Many of us don't know who lives next door to us, but we spend untold time on Facebook trying to connect with people on another continent. We're so busy and stressed that we have stopped volunteering for school groups and nonprofits that help those in need. The only time we see our neighbors is when there is a natural disaster such as a tornado, flood, fire, or bad storm.

What happens to our civilization when we don't have front porches and other forums and venues for enjoying leisure with our neighbors? A part of our humanness dies when we stop living on our front porches and stop talking, communicating, sharing, and loving one another as a community. As we continue our isolation we become negative, selfish, and apathetic.

We need a renewal of what community is. "Never doubt that a small group of thoughtful, committed citizens can change the world," said Margaret Mead. Global warming is an opportunity for each of us to rethink "community." We must come together to talk about how each community can become a beacon of hope and optimism in the midst of this global climate disaster.

Can we begin innovative recycling programs? Can we rethink water usage as a collective group? Can we have a community vegetable and flower garden or park? Can we have a community renovation program to give our community a facelift? What about a community watch program for crime?

Our daughter went to a school with brilliant teachers, but the school was dreary and in disrepair. All it would take to brighten the environment was some paint, but there were no funds to paint the classrooms that so desperately needed attention. I decided that we could organize all the parents and create a plan to shift this obstacle into an opportunity.

We made a list of each classroom, hall, office, and bathroom that needed painting. The cost of painting each space was put on a list so that families could sign up to "sponsor" a room. Some families could afford to paint an entire classroom, and others pooled resources to share the costs of one classroom. Whether it was fifty dollars or five-hundred dollars, each family contributed, and we all participated in the rehabilitation of this fine old structure. The updating provided an environment the students could be proud of, and the cooperation of their families created optimism at the school.

We can come together for myriad reasons to face any obstacle. When a neighbor has a family member in the hospital, other neighbors can rotate providing meals and mowing the lawn. When a community has lost funding for health care, professionals can volunteer services at a free clinic, and parents and other citizens can lobby legislators as loudly as any special interest group. If drunk driving and other alcohol-related crimes are a problem, form a neighborhood, city, or county group of citizens to confront the problem.

Optimism is infectious. Just beginning with some small project can plant the seed to begin great things. The energy of optimism in your neighborhood will draw people out of their homes and stimulate everyone to become active in their community. Optimism reminds us that we are one human family and that separation is an illusion.

Every obstacle becomes an opportunity. Global warming and the meltdown of our planet is just the mirror of what has happened to the meltdown of our individual selves and our families. We can begin a new paradigm of community with collaborative optimism. These tough economic times offer an opportunity for us to literally or figuratively build front porches on our homes to invite others into our lives. If you can't do that, use the town square, the city's downtown, and parks as the front porch and hold meetings and activities there.

We are one human family sharing one common destiny. We are part of the same universe, and when hope makes an impact in one part of the world, the ripple is felt all over.

BEGIN TODAY

What is my excuse for not being an agent of optimism in my community?

Ask *Your Self*

How can I create an optimistic community?

Tell *Your Self*

I am optimistic. I can contribute to my community.

Give *Your Self*

Volunteer in your community to produce positive change.

CHAPTER 21

Perseverance: The Third Commitment

> **AWARE OF THE SUFFERING CAUSED BY APATHY, IMPATIENCE, AND INDIFFERENCE, I AM COMMITTED TO PRACTICING PERSEVERANCE IN EVERY FACET OF MY LIFE.**

A tiny woman from Albania, living in India, was turned down time after time by the hierarchy of the Catholic Church in her quest to minister to the poor. But her determination was like a bulldozer in a field of cotton. She would not give up. Mother Teresa passionately loved the people who lived in the smelly, rotten poverty rampant in the gutters of Calcutta. She knew that this was her life's work, and no one could tell her otherwise or keep her from it.

On her repeated, unrelenting visits to the purple-robed bishops in a humble nun's habit she never waivered. The four-foot-ten icon became the voice for the millions who had no voice. She would not be silenced. She persevered until she received permission from the Holy See to start her own order, Missionaries of Charity, whose mission was to love and care for the rejected, for those persons no one was willing to look after or take care of. She ministered to the poorest and sickest who had gathered around her. Later she was awarded a Nobel Peace Prize and recognized as one of the most beloved and influential humans who ever lived.

Perseverance is one of the greatest attributes one can possess or acquire. Perseverance means to continue a course of action in spite of difficult opposition. Perseverance is grounded in determination and resolute purpose. Being honest and optimistic enough to overcome obstacles and having hope amid suffering requires grit, stamina, endurance, and steadfast and tenacious attention focused on hanging in, holding fast, pressing on, seeing through, toughing it out. In short, perseverance is courage.

It took Thomas Edison thousands of attempts before he discovered the lightbulb. Most people experience failure as the end. Great minds like Edison's experience failure as motivation. His potent comment on failure was "Many of life's failures are people who did not realize how close they were to success when they gave up."

The Buddhists have a saying about how to best follow the path to enlightenment: "Fall down forty times, get up forty-one." Seriously, I could just tell you to continue reading this statement over each day of your life. Repeat it each time a difficult task or situation arises. This is the unvarnished truth behind perseverance. It's simple, but it's not easy.

Some of us are born with more ability to persevere than others. Others have more stamina because they have been using their "perseverance muscles." Perseverance is like anything else: the more you exercise and practice, the better you are at it. We know now, with emerging science, that there are practices that help us learn how to become stronger in the area of perseverance. Perseverance is a discipline. When applied to every situation, perseverance is the foundation of confidence and the scaffolding for creativity.

One of the attributes of great leaders, the most inspirational people on the planet, and the holiest gurus in the universe is perseverance. All leaders have their stories of perseverance, and this is why we love and follow them.

Nelson Mandela spent twenty-seven years in prison—twenty-seven years exiled not only from his family, work, and home, but from nature, technology, and progress. He was imprisoned, but he was not enslaved. He kept his mind occupied, and not long after he was released he became president of South Africa. This was due not only to his own perseverance, but also to the commitment of all those who continued his mission to end apartheid and never forgot about him even though he was hidden away by authorities. One man's refusal to give up inspired massive resistance to the oppression by a minority of the majority and eventually the emergence of a democratic government.

RESILIENCE

Resilience is at the core of perseverance. Resilience is the ability to bounce back. Resilience allows you to recover your strength in the most distressing situations.

It is always interesting that adversity brings out the best in some and defeat in others. I have done counseling with some women who talk about how they are unable to recover after their divorce. They tell me they are still angry, can't sleep, have eating problems, and have difficulty in the job market because they gave up their education for a marriage. It always shocks me when I ask them how long ago the divorce took place, and they say, "Ten years ago." Why do some of us hold on to our suffering and become disabled while others respond to failures and disappointments with resilience and bounce back to create a dynamic life of our dreams?

There are many character traits in a person who is resilient. Some of these common traits are humor, playfulness, and curiosity. A resilient person also displays a quick adaptive response to extreme changes, experiences life as a series of challenges, brings stability to a crisis, and maintains inner calm in a stressful situation. You may have great natural resilience you were born with in your DNA, or you may have grown up with family mentors who exuded resilience. If you didn't naturally inherit resilience or grow up in a family displaying this wonderful virtue, you can learn how to become more resilient by learning and practicing disciplines that foster resilience.

RELAPSE

Even Gandhi and Mother Teresa got discouraged and agitated at times. They wouldn't be human if they didn't. The idea of perseverance is to not quit five minutes before the miracle. It is not to be on duty, ready with the shovel to dig into any situation, every minute of your life. There will be times when you need to take a break and water your soul. There will be times when you fall down that it takes longer to get back up. No one will work the Four Commitments of H.O.P.E. perfectly and consistently. The important thing is to remember that you can pick up perseverance right where you put it down.

I have experienced this scenario many times. The CNN live interview I had finished was still spinning in my head as I opened the door to our home, kicked the Prada heels off my sore feet, and threw my new jacket over the kitchen chair. Even the refrigerator door felt heavy in my exhaustion after such a monumental day, which was full of media interviews. I poured myself a glass of iced tea and fell back into our couch littered with four Jack Russells, a black lab, a retriever, and a mixed mutt. The moment was interrupted when I heard a loud thump and scratching on the back door to the dogs' room.

Our local animal shelter had ten puppies that had been in quarantine for a disease, and the shelter needed someone to take them so they could get regular medicine, good food, sunlight, exercise, and lots of love. I was fostering the puppies for a few weeks to get them better.

I rushed back, opened the door, and then slid across the floor, hit the wall, landed hard on my rear end, and smashed against the wet tile floor. I was sitting in a sea of urine and feces, disoriented and furious. There was poop between my toes and fingers from my slide. My new slacks had turned into a rag for the soiled floor. I was literally covered with excrement. I took a deep breath and quickly remembered that I had chosen this just like everything else in my life. But I was tired, it was late, and I just couldn't take care of one more thing.

I grabbed the paper towels and cleaning spray on the counter above my head and knelt on the disgusting tile floor. Out of nowhere, I was flooded with a tremendous sadness. Tears started pouring down my face, dripping into the sea of excrement. My heart was breaking. What in the hell was this about? The more I wiped away the tears and cleaned up one pile of stool after another, the more I sobbed. Then the voices began: "Why am I still cleaning up crap? I have worked hard, sacrificed, lived as good of a life as I could, and here I am still on my knees on the floor cleaning up dog crap in my St. John slacks." It was a complete meltdown. The primordial issues of my life were cycling again.

I keep forgetting what I teach others. Our core issues don't ever leave us. They cycle back again and again, just like the seasons of the year. Our job is to grow in awareness enough to know when these issues are showing up, and hopefully each time they rear their painful heads, we deal with them in a more compassionate, healthy way. It is still challenging to be as compassionate with myself as I am with others.

Obviously this was more than about puppy dog doodoo. So I allowed this enormous tsunami of pain and sadness to sweep over and through me. This trigger brought back a flood of memories: cleaning up the body parts of my cat that my father had shot with a shotgun when I was a child, washing the blood and afterbirth off me after foaling out a mare, cleaning the manure-filled stalls in the stables at six on those freezing mornings, sitting with my beloved patients as they died with the smell of death and my sense of surrender, and the constant state of washing up excrement from the many dogs we rescue, whether they are diseased or close to their death. Sitting in the middle of this squalor, I told myself again, "I chose this."

I did not choose my father's violence when I was a child, but I did choose to minister to four-leggeds and two-leggeds in their deepest woundedness. I could not put the cat back together, but I could ease the suffering of others without destroying my self.

Part of my journey down the winding river and my discovery of the spring and hope at Oak Haven was involuntary. Some of my "choices" were hardwired into my brain. I was drawn to animals. I had no desire to be dishonest, lie, and fabricate. I was an optimist in all things. And I had an unusual stamina for persevering. But the specifics were my choice. I brought the horses to Oak Haven; I accepted the puppies. There are times when I have to wade into magnificent and sacred Lake Sautee to rescue an animal, and I get stuck in the muck, in the rich silt that has accumulated on the spring side of the lake basin. Even wading through holy water, I can sink up to my waist in mud. But there has always been someone there to hear my call for help and pull me to safety. And so I do it again the next time, trusting what I know to be true.

In the next chapters we will explore the specific aspects of perseverance and how creating a new attitude can transform your life. You will learn about practicing perseverance with your self, with your partner, with the Divine, in your family, at work, and in your community.

CHAPTER 22

Perseverance with My Self

AWARE OF THE SUFFERING CAUSED BY APATHY, IMPATIENCE, AND INDIFFERENCE, I AM COMMITTED TO PRACTICING PERSEVERANCE WITH MY SELF.

What kind of person would choose to live in a tree for 738 days? A woman named Julia Butterfly Hill. She chose to live in Luna, a six-hundred-year-old California Redwood tree, to keep loggers from cutting it down. This courageous woman, by engaging in civil disobedience, not only saved Luna, the majestic tree, but alerted environmental groups about the destruction of the ancient forests of the Northwest and around the world.

On December 18, 1999, Julia climbed down from Luna a hero. Her perseverance and commitment inspired millions all over the world to persevere in the face of powerful obstacles. Day after day, month after month, season after season, she stayed up in that tree. What allowed her to keep that commitment day after day?

Perseverance is the engine that drives our lives. We are actually propelled by perseverance each day we get up out of bed, take a shower, eat, dress, and show up for work. We're all capable of persevering—doing what needs to be done to take care of our basic, daily needs. The trick is to keep persevering when we reach an obstacle.

Optimism is the fuel for perseverance. But when you run out of fuel, sometimes it's a matter of self-propulsion. Sometimes you have to drag yourself into action kicking, screaming, and crying for mercy. Once you've done that a number of times, you realize that you don't need to be so noisy. The results are worth the effort.

What role has perseverance played in your life? Think back to your school days and remember your first spelling bee, your first baseball game, your first term paper, or your first play. Did you miss the spelling of a word and never try it again, or did you decide to study harder and try to do better next time? Did you get a lower grade than you should have on your term paper and blow it off, or did you ask the teacher if you could do extra credit to bring up your grade? How much perseverance were you naturally gifted with, and how much did you learn from others or by trial and error?

Having a college education was of the utmost importance to me but of little to no importance to my parents. We were constantly moving, which made it extremely difficult to attend a college for more than a few semesters at a time. I didn't feel I could move away and attend a specific college as an independent student, because I was worried about my mother's safety, so I tried to stay close to home whenever they moved.

By the time I finished my undergraduate degree in finance, I had attended seven colleges in Florida, Ohio, Georgia, and Alabama. Each time I had to change schools, I would lose credits that wouldn't transfer. But I was determined to earn a college degree. I knew an education creates choices and an opportunity to have money and security, something I had never experienced.

Being dedicated to a goal, I persevered, never allowing my focus to waver despite the seeming lack of stability to my college "plan." I had my eye on the big picture—earning a degree so that I could get a good job and take care of myself. That provided the stability. The details would work out if I simply persevered in my educational goals.

TOOLS FOR PERSEVERANCE

Stress and depression can destroy perseverance, so it is important to learn simple stress-reduction tools. Every time my life has been turned upside down and my plans shot through with holes—after surviving the suffering (barely)—I review my lessons from the event, take a deep breath, let it go, and move on. I inherited a resilient personality, but I have also spent untold time, energy, and money learning how to enhance and tweak my natural survival skills.

One of the greatest gifts I ever gave myself was taking the time to learn how to meditate. Meditation enhances our ability to persevere. It releases the stress and pressure of any situation. Meditation allows us to unplug from people and situations and return home to ourselves. It clears the mind, slows the brain waves, cools us off, and restores a sense of balance, energy, and power. Meditation provides a remarkable root with which to anchor perseverance.

Begin today to develop perseverance in your life. Just like you would go to the gym if you wanted to build up your biceps, learn how to build up your perseverance.

I was fortunate to study with meditation masters, but many communities and organizations offer meditation or centering prayer classes, as well as classes on stress-reduction practices. Hospitals, community centers, college outreach programs, or local YMCAs may provide inexpensive classes. You can even go online to find meditation instruction.

Make sure you are exercising your body on a regular basis as well as your mind. Keeping your physical body strong feeds perseverance. Simply walking daily, taking the stairs instead of the elevator, or doing yoga a few minutes a day will help build your stamina.

Study people you admire, in history and presently alive, who lived lives of perseverance. Each person had created a variety of tools to create perseverance, and some of these will speak to you. Keep their books close to you so you can keep nourished.

Seek out workshops, seminars, and continuing education in the fields you are interested in. If you are interested in being a master gardener someday, begin by taking initial gardening classes. As you develop more confidence and experience, you will develop perseverance, courage, and confidence in your gardening skills.

Set personal goals for your life. If you want to change careers, begin by writing down your goal followed by creating your plan to create this change. When you suffer setbacks, and you will, pull out your written plan and make the needed changes. Committing your goals to paper develops your perseverance.

Share your goals and dreams for your life with those you love. Your family and friends will be your cheerleaders when you stumble or forget what's important. They will also celebrate your victories and be your blessed support system in your times of failure. Seek outside support groups to fuel your perseverance. When I was attempting to learn meditation, it was my support group of fellow meditators who taught me perseverance and gave me tips on how to persevere.

Maintaining a healthy body helps grow your perseverance. When you are rested, exercised, and healthy, you feel strong and resilient, ready to face obstacles with fortitude and courage.

No one plans to be up a creek without a paddle, but it happens. If you have provided a framework for perseverance, you will manage to row your boat home even if you have to lie down on your belly and use your hands and feet.

BEGIN TODAY

What is my excuse for not persevering in my goals for my self?

Ask *Your Self*

Am I practicing perseverance?

Tell *Your Self*

Fall down forty times, get up forty-one.

Give *Your Self*

Sign up for a meditation class in your community.

CHAPTER 23

Perseverance with the Divine

AWARE OF THE SUFFERING CAUSED BY APATHY, IMPATIENCE, AND INDIFFERENCE, I AM COMMITTED TO PRACTICING PERSEVERANCE WITH THE DIVINE.

"Religious preference?" It is always challenging for me to answer that question on forms. I hate to put one particular religion on a hospital form, because if something happened to me I wouldn't want some preacher from a church I don't know visiting me. Depending on why I'm sick, I might prefer a Buddhist monk or a Benedictine nun. I might want a shaman or meditation guru.

Some people would call me a failure for not settling on one religion. Others may say I am a success because of a lifetime of perseverance in my attempt to find a church home. I have sought the Divine in a variety of sources: Catholic, Presbyterian, United Methodist, and Episcopalian churches; Buddhism, Native American beliefs, shamanism, Kabbalism, and Taoism. Each experience led to an insufficient experience of God.

I used to feel guilty about our children not being raised in one church but exposed to many religions. Our daughter was recently going into the hospital in Salt Lake City. The admissions person asked her the same question on the admission form that drives me nuts: "What religion are you?" She smiled and confidently answered, "All of them."

Later in her room I asked her how she felt about having such a variety of religious experiences as she grew up. "I think our religious upbringing was very cool. I have had so many experiences and exposures, it makes me feel confident, and I can relate to a lot of people. I am confident in my own faith and spirituality. Mom, I had a very diverse religious upbringing."

"You didn't just show up, Mom," she said. "You deeply questioned theological texts, challenged their doctrines, and questioned their commitment to the poor. When the energy dried up, or the religion got boring, we moved to a new place. Your life has been a committed journey of perseverance to fully experience the Divine on earth. I think you are cool, Mom. Don't let anyone make you feel guilty about not joining and staying in one church your entire life. That just isn't you."

Amen.

Most other people I knew were lifelong members of a church, temple, synagogue, or mosque. Even my friends and relatives who did not like their church's views or felt they had outgrown their religion would not leave their church of origin.

There are so many people in our world who have had a difficult childhood experience with a religion, denomination, or theology. Many of us decided to allow the religious myths and damage of our childhood to destroy the possibility of an intimate relationship with the Holy. We live out old wounds and memories. There are untold Roman Catholics, Baptists, and Pentecostals whom I have seen in counseling who are enraged at their childhood religion for various policies, procedures, and experiences. I have tremendous compassion for the horrible pain and destruction these outdated theologies might have had on their lives, but the past is over. Too many people use the pain of their childhood experience to overshadow their lives now.

Perseverance is continuing a course of action in spite of the greatest suffering. Have you visited a Holocaust museum? My visit to the Holocaust Museum in Washington, D.C., is a searing memory: the bales of hair, the piles of shoes, the photos, voices of the dead and the survivors. I was haunted by my visit for years. How could any Jew ever be close to God and continue their faith in God after such human horrors? The Jews are a remarkable people who have shown their perseverance and resilience in the face of despicable horrors. They refused to allow the evil and hate of individuals to take away their God and their incredibly rich faith.

It doesn't matter what religion or nonreligion you are—please persevere in your relationship with the Divine. Your faith in something greater than yourself gives you strength and courage. If you left a traditional religion and are lost in a zone of melancholy, create something new that you believe in. Many people I know have taken the beliefs they love from some great religions and created their own faith. For example, I know many Roman Catholics who have great respect and love for Buddhism. These people follow Thich Nhat Hanh, the South Vietnamese Buddhist monk, and His Holiness the Dalai Lama, and incorporate much of this philosophy into their Catholic religious practices. I know many Jewish individuals who are also students of Buddhism and interweave many of the principles of Buddhism into their faith. I know a Hindu family who discovered the universality of Christ in their own lives and wanted to explore Christianity with a Hindu perspective.

Many religions have become dinosaurs because they decided to ignore emerging facts in science and technology. Some of us continue to stay in outdated theologies because we fear wandering into unknown spiritual or religious terrain. Rather than complain about how outdated your religion of origin is or what happened to you in your past religious experiences, get out and find a group of people who stimulate your mind and soul and try something new.

We live in a stressful world where individuals, governments, and corporations are increasingly unstable. Each of us must find peace, security, comfort, and wisdom in some experience of the Holy.

Begin to develop your own spirituality. What do you love, and what makes your heart sing? Where do you feel most connected with the Divine? How can you create time and space to grow and persevere in a long-term relationship with your spirituality?

Make your home reflect what you respect, revere, and love in our world. Your home is your sanctuary and a place to enjoy your connection with the Divine in every way. Colors can create an enlightening feeling. Filling and surrounding your home with running water, trees, plants, stones, and bird feeders, not to mention planting a simple garden, can create a constant connection with the Holy.

Create personal spiritual space in your home, in your car, and at your office. This intimate personal space can be photographs of people, pets, or places you love. Paintings, inspirational sayings, or tapestries can create a soulful environment. Keep wraps, shawls, or special blankets around to remind you of your connection with the Divine. Be creative with your personal space.

Read books on different religions and spiritualities. Create a study group for spiritual growth that meets regularly. Begin weekly home devotionals with the entire family. Read something inspirational, and discuss the reading to engage everyone's perspective. Create open discussions at your family devotions, and listen to how your children feel about the Divine. Listen deeply and encourage them to ask you questions.

Jesus told the woman at the well in Samaria that the water he was giving her was the spring of eternal life. I say perseverance is the spring of eternal hope.

BEGIN TODAY

What is my excuse for not persevering with the Divine?

Ask *Your Self*

How has the Divine shown perseverance in my own life?

Tell *Your Self*

Never, ever, ever give up.

Give *Your Self*

Go to a different spiritual or religious center for a new experience of the Divine.

CHAPTER 24

Perseverance with My Partner

> **AWARE OF THE SUFFERING CAUSED BY APATHY, IMPATIENCE, AND INDIFFERENCE, I AM COMMITTED TO PRACTICING PERSEVERANCE WITH MY PARTNER.**

"Can you hold the light for this marriage, Jim? Someone has to have the courage and strength to hold the light, and Kathleen cannot do that right now," said Joan, our marriage counselor.

We had reached that rough patch of life called "the empty nest syndrome." The kids were gone, we both had devoted enormous time and energy to our careers, and our marriage had become dry and dead. I was frustrated to my breaking point and had nothing left to give.

"Yes, I can hold the light. Kathleen has held the light for this marriage for almost thirty years, and I understand she is tired. I am ready to hold the light." In the next six months of counseling we both fell deeply in love with each other again. I have a different view of marriage than most. I think of marriage as sort of like joining the military. You join the service in the beginning, and every so many years you reenlist. Too many people make a commitment on their wedding day and slide through their marriage year after year allowing this sacred union to wither and die. Knowing how difficult a real marriage is (as opposed to the romantic fantasy), we decided from the beginning that every five years we would create a new marriage. We have actually had several incredibly rich marriages within our thirty-five-year marriage. Every five years we go to a new counselor, air our grievances and frustrations, and receive wisdom and new tools to enrich our marriage and our lives.

Every five years we recommit to new sets of responsibilities in the home. There are different stages in a family's life, and each member's needs are always shifting: the changing-diaper stage shifts to the driving-carpool era, followed by the bleacher-rash syndrome from sports, and then the teen-anxiety stage. Our marriage reflects active perseverance. Each cycle we've gone through, we clear the air and fall back in love.

The United States has the highest divorce rate in the world. Why do intelligent people repeat their wedding vows without realizing it will take perseverance to make a marriage work? When the money problems begin, the baby comes, and the infidelity creeps in, we act shocked and want out. Yet husband and wife have committed to persevere in their union for the rest of their lives.

We believe in perseverance in business, but when it comes to marriage or committed relationships we opt out too easily. There is truth in the belief that we partner with the person who will magnify where we need to grow in life. Our partner will put a spotlight on what we need to work on or heal in our lives.

When this happens, we often retreat or fight or leave the relationship in one way or another. We can leave our relationship by becoming a workaholic. We can leave the relationship by immersing ourselves in the lives of our children and ignoring the needs of our spouse. We can leave our relationship by getting involved with another person. We can leave the relationship through fostering our addictions to alcohol, drugs, or gambling. Or maybe the most painful is when we withdraw into silence and are not available emotionally, sexually, or spiritually for our partner.

I grew up in Florida, and my best friends' families were citrus farmers. The fragile fruit plants take lots of care, water, and sun. These citrus growers carefully till the soil, spend lots of time and money installing the perfect irrigation system, and plant at the perfect time of year, knowing it will take many years before the first rich crop will be harvested. They know there will be freezes, drought, extreme heat, insects, and need for workers to harvest. All of this takes a solid plan for when these obstacles occur.

Why don't we do the same for relationships? Why don't more churches, community organizations, and corporations offer courses on how to create a resilient relationship? It would benefit all of us. Divorces create untold costs to our government, corporations, children, and families.

Don't wait until your relationship is out of gas, has dirty oil, and needs the tires rotated before getting a tune-up. See a counselor. If either one of you don't like your counselor, find a new one.

Mark off your calendar for date nights, and plan to talk honestly about your relationship. Do both of you respect each other's dreams and goals? Do you both feel supported and loved? Write down five things you love for your partner to do for you. Some on my list are Jim making coffee in the morning, making a simple dinner, and rubbing my feet. It is amazing how many partners don't know what is important to each other.

Seek out the wisdom of a great therapist, marriage counselor, or sex counselor on a regular basis instead of when your relationship is falling apart. Sadly enough, most of us end up in couples counseling only when some great pain or betrayal has almost shattered our relationship.

Get out into nature with your partner. Find a common source of fun in nature. Can you both play tennis, ride horses, hike, boat, or camp? Discover a hobby you both can share and grow old together doing. When times get stressed in your relationship it is a great comfort to have created a space where you both have played together.

Celebrating eating together can be a glue for your relationship. Discover great, intimate restaurants where you know the staff and become a regular. You are creating memories and participating in a powerful, rich ritual that develops intimacy with your partner. Regularly try new restaurants and experiment with new cuisines. These small details of a relationship make life fun and exciting.

Keep fit. As we age some of us let our bodies go and don't keep up a healthy lifestyle. You will feel more sexual, attractive, and powerful if you keep your body fit. You may want to exercise or work out with your partner on a regular basis. My husband and I have had a thirty-minute walking ritual after supper for our entire marriage. We share our busy day with each other, talk about our children and family issues, and immerse ourselves in the beauty of nature. Find something that works for both of you and stick to it.

Your home is your nest and a source of great joy and happiness. A clean and orderly home creates grounding and a sense of safety. Discuss what styles of home decoration you both enjoy and love. Share your thoughts on home design and landscaping. You are building a life together, and integrating your ideas will create a resilient home that will be a source of power and grounding in the tough times.

Share your beliefs with your partner on your faith, religion, or spirituality. Life is very difficult, and sharing your faith with your partner is crucial for a long-term relationship. Practicing meditation, doing yoga, worshiping, or studying your faith together will bring strength and resilience in your relationship and in your life. Life is filled with great losses and suffering, and a shared belief system can be a life saver.

When the going gets tough and the waves are rough, paddle like hell to get to each other. You might get wet, but you both might need a thorough cleansing. Let the source of your love resurface.

BEGIN TODAY

What is my excuse for not persevering in my relationship?

Ask *Your Self*

Are we using all the tools we can to persevere in our relationship?

Tell *Your Self*

I will grow in perseverance in this relationship.

Give *Your Self*

Do a relationship tune-up by making a commitment to see a counselor.

CHAPTER 25

Perseverance with My Family

AWARE OF THE SUFFERING CAUSED BY APATHY, IMPATIENCE, AND INDIFFERENCE, I AM COMMITTED TO PRACTICING PERSEVERANCE WITH MY FAMILY.

I had never been called to do an exorcism of a home before. The woman who called me was concerned something demonic was living in her home. Growing up Catholic this concept wasn't foreign to me, but in our modern world it is rare. I was rather intrigued to check out the situation.

The door slowly opened to the small cottage home with blue shutters in this beautiful neighborhood. There stood a pale, disheveled woman with a newborn infant in her arms. "Are you Reverend Hall?"

"Yes."

"I'm Michelle Grant. Please come in." She invited me to sit down on her couch, sat beside me, and began to cry.

She was shaking, and I heard a little girl's voice from another room calling, "Mommy, Mommy, Mommy." I jumped up and walked into the kitchen, and there was a three-year-old girl sitting in her booster chair, and covered with oatmeal. I grabbed a paper towel and cleaned her up. "My name is Abby. What's your name?" she said.

"I'm Miss Kathleen." I slipped her feet on the floor, grabbed her hand, and headed back to the living room couch. "What's going on, Michelle?" I asked the woman.

"I don't know where to start. Lilly is just six weeks old. Abby is three years old and has a brain tumor. The doctors said her brain tumor is rare. They said she won't be alive in a year." Michelle broke down crying. "My husband just couldn't take it, and he walked out last week. The girls and I are alone."

I reached over and took Lilly in my arms as Abby sat close beside me. After Michelle stopped crying she began with her story again.

"This house is possessed. We moved in here a year ago. Everything has gone wrong since we moved into this home. I feel there is some presence in here. It has made Abby get cancer and my husband leave us. I feel it, I know it's here."

After a few minutes of silence I asked, "Michelle, what would you like me to do?"

"Please do an exorcism and get this evil spirit out of here. Please, please help me."

I spent the afternoon with Michelle and her girls. She was understandably overwhelmed and distraught. I was really concerned for her mental state. An exorcism of a home was not something I had ever considered before. I was very uncomfortable with Michelle's request, but her desperation concerned me greatly. I decided it would at least give her peace of mind if I blessed the house and exorcised anything not of God from her home.

The next morning I returned with holy water. The four of us went through the house slowly as I blessed each room. She was by my side as if I were protecting her in this horrible time of betrayal, abandonment, and grief. Michelle was calmer after our ritual. She felt a peace fall over her home and was convinced the evil was gone. We had coffee as I listened to her agonizing situation and helped her with her two daughters. She felt one demon in her life was gone and she was a little safer.

Over the next weeks we became friends, and I helped her go to the hospital and manage the girls on the days Abby went for chemotherapy. Sitting with Michelle as we saw the tumor on the scan was devastating. I would sit with the doctor as he told Michelle there was little chance Abby would survive.

"Would you take us to healing services at churches?" Michelle asked. "I believe in healing services, and there could be a miracle. Please, Kathleen, will you take Abby to a healing service?"

"Of course I will, Michelle. Let me find some places where they do healing services."

The next weeks were spent shepherding Michelle, Abby, and little Lilly to a variety of healing services. Poor little Abby was so weak, constantly sick and deteriorating by the day, I had to carry her while Michelle held Lilly. We were quite a team. Our first healing service was at the Episcopalian church followed by a Catholic service the next week. The one that Abby loved was the healing service at the Christian Charismatic church. The ministers danced, sang, and called people down front to be healed.

The four of us marched up to the ministers, and they prayed over Abby, anointed her, and then played some upbeat Christian music. They gave Abby an audiocassette of the healing service so she could play it over and over in her bed at home. Abby loved the tape. I bought her a little pink tape player so she could listen to it often.

Then everything changed. Michelle was more in control and grounded. Abby's face had more color, she began eating again, and she was laughing. On our next visit to the hospital the doctor rushed into the hospital room and said there was something very different going on, and he looked panicked.

"Michelle, I don't know what has happened. Abby's brain tumor was the size of a grapefruit, fast-growing, and terminal. We just did her brain scan, and the tumor is half the size it was last month. I've called in our team, and we have confirmed the tumor is getting smaller," said the doctor.

"It's a miracle! It's a miracle, Dr. Dalton! It's a miracle, Kathleen!" Michelle jumped up and hugged both of us.

The four of us headed home with this miraculous news. We were going to get some more diapers from home and celebrate with lunch out. As we drove into the driveway there was a silver SUV parked in the garage.

"It's Steve. My God, it's Steve, my husband," yelled Michelle. *Holy crap*, I thought. *What in the world was going on?* At that moment Steve walked out of the house toward my car. Abby squealed when she saw her dad and jumped out of the car and ran to her dad and sprang into his arms.

Steve had decided to come back to his family. Michelle was furious in the beginning, but after some counseling over the next weeks the family integrated again. Abby's brain tumor kept shrinking until it disappeared. I don't know if you believe in miracles, but I do.

Was there something in Michelle's home? I don't know. Did the rock-and-roll healing service heal Abby? I don't know. Why did Michelle's husband come home that particular day? I don't know.

Michelle and Steve's marriage is still strong. Abby plays on the middle school's basketball team, and Lilly is an adorable little piano player. This family has persevered against all odds and has gained strength and courage through the years.

Financial challenges, fractured marital relationships, addictions, and mental and physical illnesses can destroy a family, but the family that lives and breathes perseverance will survive even the most difficult situations.

PARENTAL GUIDE TO PERSEVERANCE

Every day more parents live in a state of what I call "overwhelmed parenting." These parents feel powerless in an environment where not just the family system is at the breaking point, but so is the world. It amazes me how many parents I hear say their children are different today. They feel there is nothing they can do about how their family is not communicating. The family is all going in different directions. By the time everyone gets home, no one has much energy left to confront children and make demands. In my work I use the term "overbooked, overworked, and overwhelmed."

It is sad when families throw in the towel. It is our responsibility to restore hope and perseverance in the family unit. This is best done with open, vulnerable communication. Communication is the essential hub of the family that has eroded. The best way to encourage communication in a family is to use some of the following tools and not let our hurried world suck the richness and love out of our families.

Parents are competing with the noise of video games, iPods, MySpace, Facebook, other Internet sites, television, and cell phones. There is a lot of communication out there, but it is not happening between you and your child, nor is it the kind of communication that will motivate and inspire your child.

Begin weekly family meetings that are mandatory for everyone to attend. Set the stage that these meetings are fun times of motivation and encouragement. These are the times parents talk to each child and become their cheerleaders.

Teach perseverance in your family by being vulnerable and talking about your day at work and your losses and gains in life. You are your children's greatest mentor. They look up to you, and it is your responsibility to not only foster their respect but to also model what is real. It's not a bad thing for children to know that their parents are working hard for the family rather than buying themselves a new car or an expensive outfit.

It is frustrating being a parent in our stressful world. We need more support and information than ever before. You can investigate local parenting courses at your community center or at your local church, synagogue, or temple. Seek parental support groups. They are a great source of information and mental health. Other parents with the same challenging problems can shed light on your situation and be a source of great support. There is lots of great information online these days. Investigate parenting Web sites. They are a great place to get information and referrals and discover community.

If you are dealing with a chronic illness of a family member, a long-term challenge such as ADHD, or a serious condition such as depression of a family member, you need to seek professional help for continued support. We are living in an age of specialists and experts who are glad to guide you the through difficult waters of demanding situations.

Learn to be a great listener. Many parents just "send" to their children and do not "receive." Children know when you are present and compassionately listening to their stories and experiences. Practice listening as if your life depended upon it. Listening is one of the greatest skills in life. When you listen to people you are showing them that they are valued, respected, and loved.

The gift of creating a resilient family is that no matter what crisis develops, you will weather the storm and reap the benefits of greater communication and love. Believe in the sanctity of your family. Do what you need to do to protect that. Then get up the next day and do the same thing. Endure. Enjoy. Persevere.

BEGIN TODAY

What is my excuse for not persevering in family relationships?

Ask *Your Self*

How can I teach my children perseverance?

Tell *Your Self*

I am the living example of perseverance in my family.

Give *Your Self*

For fifteen minutes every night turn off all technology.

CHAPTER 26

Perseverance with My Work

AWARE OF THE SUFFERING CAUSED BY APATHY, IMPATIENCE, AND INDIFFERENCE, I AM COMMITTED TO PRACTICING PERSEVERANCE WITH MY WORK.

At one of our favorite restaurants, we picked up the menu to order our usual red snapper as Diane walked up to our table with her pad and pen. Looking up to order, I noticed her eyes were puffy, as if she had been crying.

"Hi, Diane. Are you OK?" I asked.

Her bottom lip was quivering as she said, "You know I've had this restaurant here for twenty years. I have worked like a dog to keep this place going. It's hard for a woman to own a restaurant and run it by herself.

"I got a call from the man I lease this building from, and he is going to sell this old building to some rich developer who can pay him more than I could ever afford. I don't know where I can move my restaurant. The property around here is so expensive, I would have to move away from all my customers." Diane began to cry. I reached over and held her hand.

"Diane, you are a strong woman and have owned your own restaurant for a long time. Stick in there, something good will happen to you. If we can help, let us know."

It was a couple of months before we ate at Diane's restaurant again. As we walked in we saw Diane standing at the kitchen door. She was smiling and looked energetic and happy. "Hi, Diane. You look great. What's new with you?" I asked.

"In twenty years I have had chefs walk out on me, my husband died, the usual stress of running a busy restaurant, but having them throw me out of this space broke my heart. Guess what? Since I saw you last, the real estate market has crashed, and the developer dropped his offer. So I get to keep this place. I am so happy."

Diane's face was glowing. This woman had persevered in her business every day of her life. No matter what life dealt her, she got stronger. We have been at her restaurant when the wait staff didn't show, and she was there washing tables, delivering food, cooking in the kitchen. She lives perseverance daily.

LIVE YOUR PASSION

People like Diane love their work and experience pride and dignity in it. Her passion is contagious. But these days I don't meet many people who love what they do.

A recent survey reported over 70 percent of employees said they did not like the company they worked for and did not like their work. This is staggering. Do employees increasingly dislike their jobs because corporations have less loyalty for their staff? Or are people seeking more meaning in their lives because of this frenzied world and they feel like pawns in the demand of corporate profits?

It is difficult to enjoy perseverance at work when you don't like or respect the company you work for. Respect for your employer is paramount but it's impossible if you don't feel respected.

If you don't like your job but have to keep it for benefits, that is understandable. Many of us have to have insurance benefits and retirement for our families. You can plant a seed of hope even in the direst of circumstances.

While you are keeping this job, as you have to feed and support your family, change your attitude. Be grateful for the food it puts on your table and the health insurance it provides your family. After work, begin to plant the seeds of your passion. If you love gardening, take an evening course in gardening or landscaping. If you love building and want to begin a career as a tile expert or painter, learn how at a local home improvement store that offers night or weekend classes. If your dream is to be a teacher or a nurse, take weekend courses at a local community college.

Yes, it may be a little difficult balancing everything at the beginning, but soon you will experience the joy of doing what you love, and that is all that matters. You will develop perseverance at your job because you have a ray of hope and are watering the seeds of your dream.

If you have a job you already love, learn how to be more resilient at work. Many corporations do not have adequate work-life balance programs. Some corporations do not have flexible working hours or job sharing. You can be the person to introduce these innovative ideas to your corporation. Be positive and armed with the new research on how corporations with work-life balance programs reap the rewards on their bottom lines. We know that employee work-life balance programs result in less employee turnover, more productivity, higher creativity on the job, and reduced health-care costs. Your boss will sense your confidence and perseverance, and you will make a difference.

Perseverance is crucial if you are between jobs. Not having a job is one of the most stressful experiences in our lives. Perseverance is your best friend. Write down what nourishes you each day: a good meal, devotional time, your family, exercise, gardening, or reading. During this time of stress be sure you persevere in caring for your mental, spiritual, and physical health. Find new ways to network with others. Show up to community events and volunteer at organization functions, especially when you don't feel like it. Keep making contacts and persevere. I promise your perseverance will pay off eventually.

Don't forget to expand your horizons of what you can do for your career. Be flexible and explore new careers. When ten people show up for a job interview and you are the one who has the gift of perseverance, you will reap the rewards.

Listen to your inner voice—it will guide you. Perseverance is when you commit your life to listening to your voice within over and over and over again like the rhythm of the waves.

BEGIN TODAY

What is my excuse for not persevering with my work?

Ask *Your Self*

How can I inspire perseverance at work?

Tell *Your Self*

I will continue to work with passion and honesty every day.

Give *Your Self*

Engage a motivational speaker to speak at your company.

CHAPTER 27

Perseverance with My Community

> ## AWARE OF THE SUFFERING CAUSED BY APATHY, IMPATIENCE, AND INDIFFERENCE, I AM COMMITTED TO PRACTICING PERSEVERANCE WITH MY COMMUNITY.

Nancy moved to a new neighborhood, and it didn't have a neighborhood watch program like she had in her previous one. She talked to neighbors and brought up the subject. The neighbors blew her off. Nancy was agitated and frustrated. She got sick of complaining about how backward this neighborhood was. But instead of giving up, she decided to persevere.

Nancy made brochures on her computer and invited the neighborhood to her home for a one-hour evening meeting with brownies and coffee. About half of the people she invited showed up. Nancy made a presentation of the benefits of a neighborhood watch program, such as less crime, safer streets, and a closer-knit community.

She spearheaded the project and within two months had a very successful neighborhood program, which was the first time the neighborhood had ever come together. Nancy decided to try another experiment. She asked the group in the neighborhood watch program to have a July Fourth neighborhood party in her backyard. They formed committees to organize the food and entertainment. This subsequently went off very well, and even more people in the neighborhood showed up.

Five years later, the neighborhood is completely different due to Nancy's perseverance. Now they not only have the neighborhood watch program, but they also have neighborhood parties twice a year, and they have a network of older people in the neighborhood who call and check on the young children who get home from school with no parents in the home.

Nancy was determined to find or create community wherever she lived her life. She demonstrated the power of investing in your neighborhood to other families, who can now take that lesson with them should she or they move to a new community. She has woven a tapestry of people together who never would have known one another without her.

We moved to the mountains many years ago. I had training in mind-body medicine and had two postgraduate degrees, but there was no place in the mountains to use my expertise and training. There was a cardiopulmonary rehabilitation program, but there was no stress-reduction component in the hospital-based initiative.

I met with the physician who ran the program, and he told me there was no money to hire me and the program was hardly alive. I decided to volunteer my time to facilitate the stress-reduction program and see what could happen. Over the years there have been thousands of people who have received training and education through this program. Many times it held on by a thread, but perseverance kept it alive and thriving. Follow your passion and hold fast to your commitment.

PLANTING SEEDS OF PERSEVERANCE IN THE COMMUNITY

There are so many needs in the community where you live. Just look around your community. Read the local newspaper, watch the local television station, and listen to your local radio station. You will discover needs that you were meant to give your time to. The other gift you will receive is the amazing friends you will meet. There will be people you would never choose to be your friend working next to you with the same goal, and both of your lives become transformed.

What do you love to do? Discover what you love to do and join a group that loves the same things. A community of like-minded individuals striving for the same goals is the essence of perseverance. I love dogs, so I belong to rescue groups and foster animals. When I get tired or frustrated, my co-volunteers help me to persevere. Beth is a master gardener in our neighborhood. She is so passionate about gardening, she began a community garden where all the families in the neighborhood can share working and harvesting the vegetables.

You can engage people by putting a notice on their front door announcing a bring-your-own-basket picnic in your backyard. If there doesn't seem to be much interest, you may want to send out a questionnaire to the neighbors. Ask them what they would like to see as a community activity or get-together. Offer them choices such as meeting at a holiday time when most people are off from work, or getting together to make homemade ice cream, or a bring-your-own-covered-dish supper, or a piñata party for the kids. Be creative and be persistent. Also, don't go it alone. Get a team together to head the project. It's more fun and you get more great input.

All great community transformation in our world has been the product of great perseverance. Nothing great is ever done overnight. It is done over time, with the rhythm and energy of perseverance.

BEGIN TODAY

What is my excuse for not practicing perseverance with my community?

Ask *Your Self*

Why don't I get involved in my community?

Tell *Your Self*

I must be a visionary in my community.

Give *Your Self*

Go to one community meeting with like-minded people.

CHAPTER 28

En-Joy! The Fourth Commitment

AWARE OF THE SUFFERING CAUSED BY ANGER, VIOLENCE, AND GRIEF, I AM COMMITTED TO CULTIVATING JOY IN EVERY FACET OF MY LIFE.

When I think of joy, three people come to mind immediately: Thich Nhat Hanh, Bishop Desmond Tutu, and His Holiness the Dalai Lama. Being blessed to have studied with each has given me firsthand experience witnessing joy, which comes from inner peace, being one with the universe.

Thich Nhat Hanh, the Buddhist monk who was nominated for the Nobel Peace Prize, believes joy is the cessation of suffering. To be in his presence and listen to his gentle, reassuring words is to feel shelter from the storms. His joy is peaceful and profound and is the basis for his vast library of books and writings. His joy has a healing energy that soothes, revitalizes, and comforts: peace with every step, as he teaches.

One of the basic spiritual practices I learned from Thich Nhat Hanh is a simple smile. He believes when you live in the world with a warm smile every day, you bring joy to yourself and others. He says,

"Sometimes your joy is the source of your smile, but sometimes your smile can be the source of your joy." Try it—not as a mask to sorrow and pain, but as an act of faith and hope. It is powerful and energizing.

Bishop Desmond Tutu has an infectious smile and an exuberant personality. He literally vibrates with the energy of pure joy. He is openhearted and revels in the freedom of making and keeping personal connections. A person cannot sit beside Bishop Tutu without being transformed.

Each day in graduate school when I walked away from a lecture by Bishop Tutu, I felt as if the composition of my body, mind, and soul had changed in some mystical manner. The key to emitting this pure joy energy is cultivating the ability to detach from the emotions that prevent joy—anger, fear, worry, and apathy. Desmond Tutu never allowed the tremendous suffering and anger of racism, bigotry, and hatred to attach to his soul. He transmuted the darkness of his experiences with apartheid and radiates light. He absorbs the world through his sense of curiosity about humans and the Divine. Instead of getting angry about the world's inadequate answers to grave problems, he keeps questioning us, leading us to solutions that will benefit everyone.

His Holiness the Dalai Lama glides across space with an impish smile on his soft face and a radiance surrounding him. He is eternally amused, pregnant with laughter. At any moment he may break into giggles, yet in the next moment he can tell a short story with passion and clarity. The Dalai Lama does not allow violence, anger, and political anguish to affect his mission on this earth. His disciplined spiritual practices keep His Holiness rooted in joy at all times. He may be exalted by followers of Tibetan Buddhism and admired by the world community, but he is a very humble man, who finds happiness in his routines of meditation and study. He teaches that the highest wisdom is kindness—to yourself as well as others.

What can we learn from these individuals? They demonstrate that a life of joy is connected to awareness, engagement, meditation, prayer, mindfulness, dietary disciplines, community, and devotion.

But you must begin with the intention of wanting to experience joy. Most of us hope or pray that joy will turn up in our lives. We think of it as partying out loud or something that pops into our lives like fireworks that explode overhead, sending streaks of light across the sky. Those fleeting moments are not joy. They're exciting, stimulating, and fun. But they are transitory jolts of happiness.

Joy is a state of grace in which we experience communion with our selves and the Divine. Joy is an internal calm, a feeling that despite all the raging storms around us, inside all is well.

We think we know what will make us happy: success, fame, money, beauty, power, or intelligence. All of these attributes are wonderful, but I can assure you, as one who humbly can say I have had the privilege of all of these, they don't manifest joy, diminish suffering, or create peace in your life. Medicating our depression, dissatisfaction, disorientation, and disease with possessions, distractions, drama, and diversions is not the answer we seek. We can justify and rationalize the necessity of all these things, but joy is an inside job.

We all have the seeds of joy within us, but if we don't water, nourish, and tend our joy, it is difficult to know it is there. It can be cultivated by living mindfully and by continually developing our awareness.

Once you decide to commit to bliss, you have no choice but to live differently. You consciously choose what to allow into your body and mind. You are mindful of your senses when you eat. You move intentionally. You learn to control the flow of noisy thoughts and be discriminating in what you choose to read, watch on TV, or hear from others. You want less. You find fulfillment in wholeness and small pleasures. You rejoice in the rhythm of breathing and can slow down your heartbeat and feel the pulse of the earth.

If life is suffering, how can Buddhists or Jews or Catholics or any of us live in joy? By fearlessly accepting the suffering instead of running away from it or trying to disguise it. Suffering hurts. It is painful. But it is part of the human condition. How could we know the release and pleasure of a belly laugh if we did not know the painful tug of gut-wrenching grief and uncontrollable tears? Joy does not exist in a vacuum or bubble. It is not mindless happiness or an exaggerated sense of pleasure. It is earned by committing to experience the full spectrum of the human condition. You can find it just by sitting in contemplation for twenty minutes a day. You can spread it by showing the face of joy to all whom you meet in your daily life.

Hope energy—honesty, optimism, and perseverance—will lead you to en-joy, living in joy. It is a natural flow. You've traveled the river, settled by the spring. Joy will bring you home every day of your life no matter where you are.

Joy is present in each element of H.O.P.E. When you live a life rooted in honesty, you experience joy. Optimism is living a daily diet of joy. Perseverance makes you feel strong and joyful. Joy is infused in every facet of H.O.P.E.

The following chapters will teach you how to instill joy into every facet of your life. You will learn how to permeate your self with joy, create joy with your partner, experience joy with the Divine, fill your family with joy, saturate your workplace with joy, and impart joy in your community.

CHAPTER 29

En-Joy My Self

> **AWARE OF THE SUFFERING CAUSED BY ANGER, VIOLENCE, AND GRIEF, I AM COMMITTED TO CULTIVATING JOY WITH MY SELF.**

She was short and stocky with stooped shoulders. Her Coke-bottle glasses slid down on her large nose. She seemed to be in her sixties. She shuffled through the crowd gathered around her as if she were a rock star. The service had just ended as I sat at the back of the historic Presbyterian church in the Sautee Valley wondering who this beloved person was.

Our family regularly visited various churches to explore their theologies, ministers, and parishioners. We had driven past this beautiful historic church in the Cherokee Valley and that Sunday had decided to check it out. The moment the minister finished the benediction, people jumped up and stampeded toward this woman.

We had gathered our things and were heading to our car when I felt someone touch me on the shoulder. "Hi. Welcome to our church. I am Ruth Bonner." The most popular woman at church extended her hand, and I introduced our family. She continued, "Would love to get to know you. May I call you and invite you for coffee at my home?"

No one had ever invited me to their home so soon after meeting them. I fumbled for words and then said, "Sure, I'd love to have coffee with you." After giving her my number we headed home. The next day she called with directions to her home and asked me to come for coffee on Wednesday at nine in the morning. I was intrigued and excited.

I checked the address Ruth had given me several times as I sat in her driveway, staring at the olive green house with red shutters. It stuck out like a single blooming rose in the brambles of common white clapboard structures. This place was a reflection of some kind of bold personality. Who was this woman?

As I hit the top step, I noticed a beautiful flowered tray sitting on a green wicker table on the front porch. Gorgeous lavender hydrangeas were in a small vase in the middle of the tray, and I recognized one of my favorite bone china patterns on the tray, Kutani Crane by Wedgwood. Ruth had meticulously matched the lavender in the hydrangeas with the lavender cranes painted on the cups and lavender linen napkins under the sterling silver teaspoons. I could already feel a sense of mindfulness, love, kindness, and intention.

I rang the doorbell and waited as her feet pounded to the front door. "Hi, Kathleen, you hold this plate of cranberry oat muffins I just made. Be careful, they're hot, and I have the coffee here. Let's go sit down and celebrate this glorious morning." Every detail had been attended to: the aromatic fresh ground coffee with real cream, and, from her mother's recipe, warm homemade muffins—laced with huge scarlet cranberries and served with sweet, soft butter—that melted in my mouth.

Ruth tenderly questioned me about the usual details one wants to know about a stranger: spouse, children, career, where I lived, and previous religious affiliations. Leaning forward, she paid intense attention to each detail of my life as she continued to fill my cup with warm coffee, smiling reassuringly.

The hours flew by as she talked of her ten-year battle with breast cancer, surrendering one breast at a time over the years. Her husband had left her, and her daughter had abandoned her many years before. But there was a sense of peace and acceptance with every word she uttered. No anger, no despair, no sadness, just pure joy exuding in every word and movement of her body.

That was my initial glimpse into this woman's holiness and how she helped to make others whole. Little did I know she would be one of the "Ammas," or sacred mothers, of my life, teaching me how to discover joy in each moment.

Our relationship moved from glorious coffee and tea rituals to remarkable lunches at her home. She was a woman of the Old South. Lunch was a major formal meal that included garden vegetables, homemade angel flake biscuits with butter and homemade preserves, brewed iced tea with mint, formal china, linens, and a delicious homemade pie or cake for dessert. Ruth knew the joy of planting, cooking, preserving, and feasting on wondrous food.

Many of our evenings were spent walking through her garden filled with hydrangeas, heirloom roses, peonies, clematis, and day lilies. Her joy energy was fertilizer to not only the plants but to all of creation. On our long walks she said hi to every bug, bird, plant, dog, cat, and tree.

Ruth taught me that each of us is born into joy, but we allow the suffering and obstacles in our lives to strip us of who we really are. She said joy is our God-given gift. I learned from Ruth that joy is the Divine, essential, vital energy of life, and we must nurture it, feed it, respect it, and be joy in the world.

Ruth was a magnet to every animal, human, and plant. Everything grew, healed, and laughed in her presence. Every type of person imaginable attended Ruth's funeral: senators, CEOs, homeless people, children, farmers, carpenters, and her car mechanic. All of us celebrating her life had the same story. Her joy had transformed each person.

CREATING JOY IN SIMPLE WAYS

Few people these days really know what the definition of joy is, and many think it must be shared to exist. But the foundation of joy begins with you and the simple and ordinary moments of your life.

A necessary preliminary step is cultivating the ability to rest. People are not getting enough sleep today. Keep your bedroom cool and invest in dark curtains or shades. Reading is transporting and a good transition activity to end the day. Try to have only one book at a time by your bed—but not a thriller. Make sure your blanket or comforter is soft and light. We are creatures to whom touch is important. There is something delicious about crawling into bed with crisp, clean sheets. Store your rosary or other reminders of prayer and affirmation in a beautiful container on the bed stand—whether stones with a single word carved on them or note cards and letters you have received and like to reread. When we rest we restore and renew our mind, body, and soul. Sleeping is holy and makes us whole.

When you awaken, start using your five senses as portals for experiencing joy. Take an extra ten minutes for your morning shower. Feel the water pinging your skin. See the individual drops. Listen to the streams of water hitting the tile. Smell your favorite bath soap or body lotion. Try vanilla, lavender, or peppermint. On cold days, warm your towel in the dryer before wrapping yourself up in it. Know that you are preparing your body for the day, and be grateful for modern conveniences like water heaters.

Create a tea or coffee ritual, whether in the morning or at a break time. You don't have to rely on your usual caffeine pit stop every day. At least once a week, use your favorite china, napkins, and a tray to serve yourself. Say a prayer of thanks before sipping, and note how it deepens your pleasure to slow down. Actually taste what's in your cup.

Spend time outdoors every day. In temperate climates, gardening promotes communion with Mother Earth and the cycles of nature. Sowing seeds is a great source of joy as we witness how planting a tiny jot of hope results in a kaleidoscope of colors, flavors, and scents.

What do you love to listen to? Each of us has our favorite music. Make sure you keep it close to you on an iPod, CD, or your computer. If you love nature sounds, purchase an alarm clock that wakes you with the sound of the ocean, a babbling brook, the wind, or a rainstorm. It might take a little extra time each day to tune in to what turns on your joy. But don't deprive yourself of the sounds you love.

When you shower yourself with sensory experiences, you wash away worry, distraction, fear, stress, and depression.

In addition, carve out a few minutes for play each day. Sometimes I sing to the dogs or dance around the room with my broom to "Bibbidi-Bobbidi-Boo" from Disney's *Cinderella*.

Riding my wild mare is like riding the wind. That is a time that I belly laugh and tell her how much I love her for giving me more joy than I thought I could ever experience.

I love to lie outside at night and watch the stars, pretending some talking bear or gentle deer will emerge from the woods and let me touch it. How can you experience and enjoy your playful nature?

Lying on the porch with my dogs is a simple pleasure that lights up my day. When I surrender to the furry pile of canines and experience the thrill of their hearts beating in a rhythmic cadence, their panting, and their enthusiastic licking, I feel as if I am in the middle of a symphony of audible sensory joy.

Another place of perfect joy for me is sitting near my bird feeder and becoming one with the birds singing, eating, and flitting around my porch. The cardinals, goldfinches, indigo buntings, and brown thrashers lift me into heaven with the beating of their wings. I feel full to bursting but light on my feet—which is how joy feels, as if you're going to start singing or flying like a bird.

Joy transports even as it is grounding—like water in rivers, springs, and oceans. Like ripples that spread from a single drop. When you choose to live in joy, you move with the flow of the Divine.

BEGIN TODAY

What is my excuse for not experiencing joy in my life?

Ask *Your Self*

How can I begin to experience more joy today?

Tell *Your Self*

I experience joy in my life.

Give *Your Self*

Spend some time in nature—sit by a river or stream—and experience joy.

CHAPTER 30

En-Joy the Divine

AWARE OF THE SUFFERING CAUSED BY ANGER, VIOLENCE, AND GRIEF, I AM COMMITTED TO CULTIVATING JOY WITH THE DIVINE.

"Pass the salt, please," said the petite red-haired woman sitting beside me. I handed her the salt shaker, and she smiled and said, "Thank you so much. I am Sister Julian."

I had checked into the monastery three days before and had heard about the monastery's hermit, Sister Julian. Others had warned me it would be a rare sighting, but if I were lucky I might meet her. I felt blessed she was eating next to me at the large round table with six other nuns. I was on a quest for answers, so I was filled with so many questions I didn't know where to start.

Sister Julian told me her gift was to live alone as a hermit and devote her life completely to God, undistracted. She spent her time tending to the monastery's gardens, which provided the fresh vegetables and flowers to the monastery. When she wasn't gardening, she spent part of her day crocheting afghans to help create income for the monastery.

Her famous afghans were sold at county fairs and by special order to visitors at the monastery. She spent the rest of her day in devotion to the Divine in meditation and prayer.

Sister Julian manifests joy to all who are privileged to be in her presence. Isolated at the hermitage, she fills herself up with joy in her daily devotions and tending tasks, and it spills over into everything she encounters at the monastery and the world. I bought one of her afghans, made from leftover yarn from all of her prized afghans. Every time I wrap myself in it, I am warmed by her joy and reminded that our charge in this world is to be joy.

DIVINE JOY

Do you en-joy your experience with the Holy, or does it feel like mandatory exercise, discipline, or even punishment? Many of us feel as though we have lost our soul when we try to experience the Divine. We are dutiful but not joyful in the presence of the Divine.

Some of us were taught to fear God because if you anger the Holy you may end up in the fires of hell. (By the way, I don't believe in hell.) Some experience Jesus as the serious, suffering Jesus rather than a curious, brilliant, compassionate, articulate man who was a master storyteller with a great sense of humor. How can people experience joy with a judgmental God whom they fear?

If you want to experience God as a God of Joy, witness the wondrous sunset over the mountains. Listen to the rain fall on the roof and beat on the windowpanes, and immerse yourself in the smell of the fresh rain on the pastures.

The joy of the Divine is present when you stand in a stable and witness the birth of a foal and watch her try to stand and take her first step. Smile with the Holy as you return home late from work, exhausted and frustrated, open the front door, and are greeted with a big lick and a tail intensely wagging. In that moment of adoration and acceptance, there is a peace and love beyond description. These are the simple moments of life when the Holy intersects with our busy lives and says, "En-Joy."

Love rests in the center of joy and the Divine. Loving another person is the incarnation of Divine joy. I believe, as many scriptures say, each of us is *imago dei*, created in the image of God. As we love our selves and others we experience the joy of the Divine. Examine your relationships with friends, family, and coworkers, and be aware that the joy you receive and give in these holy relationships makes you whole.

When you feel frustrated with organized religion or too tired to participate in the rituals you feel you should perform, visit your own altar. Pick a spot in your home where you can create a special devotional space with your favorite inspirational books, a candle, and a place to sit. When you trust and frequent this sacred space, it will be a place where you will experience the joy of meeting with the Divine. When you bring yourself to the shore, it's more likely that you will immerse yourself in the water than if you don't show up at all.

The Divine is a source of pure joy. I invite you to open your heart to the infinite opportunities to experience joy with the Divine. Whether it is in a glorious lavender sunset over the ocean, the purring of your cat on your chest, the body of your partner or child against yours, or at the altar of your local worship center, seize the joy!

BEGIN TODAY

What is my excuse for not experiencing Divine joy?

Ask *Your Self*

What characteristics do I associate with the Divine?

Tell *Your Self*

I experience joy when I connect with the Divine.

Give *Your Self*

Read a book of inspirational sayings.

CHAPTER 31

En-Joy My Partner

AWARE OF THE SUFFERING CAUSED BY ANGER, VIOLENCE, AND GRIEF, I AM COMMITTED TO CULTIVATING JOY WITH MY PARTNER.

"This marriage won't work." That's what Jenny, our marriage counselor, said to us two weeks after our fifteenth wedding anniversary. "You are both living in a desert. You haven't watered your marriage with joy, and it has become barren. You have put your children and careers and your to-do lists before each other."

We sat at opposite ends of the couch, arms folded across our chests, legs crossed, with little eye contact. We are both type-A people and had allowed our marriage to take a backseat to our busy lives. As much as we had tried to blame each other, we both had to take responsibility for the death of joy in our lives. But how could we get it back? Could it be revived?

"Begin by making a list of ten things you would love to have your spouse do that brings you joy," suggested Jenny. It seemed strange that we had never thought of doing this before. I guess we assumed that we knew what brought the other person joy, but we had not asked each other.

Jim's list began with horseback riding, eating long lunches together, me sitting in the bathroom while he shaved, and riding on the golf cart with him when he fed the horses. I was so touched by his list. My list was Jim making me coffee in the morning, sitting on the bench talking to me as I take my bath, reading to me at night, and taking walks together.

This simple, ordinary exercise put joy, energy, and love back into our marriage. Spending this intimate time together planted the seeds of joy in our marriage. Once we experienced pure joy with each other, we made sure we made "joy time" essential. Everything changes when you root your marriage in joy. Communication, sex, laughter, raising children, stress, and depression: it all transforms when you commit to "joy time." That was twenty years ago, and we both know it saved our marriage.

JOY IS THE GLUE

One of the basic purposes of an intimate relationship is to share joy. Marriage is supposed to be an institution of joyfulness. It is sad that so many of us experience only fleeting moments of joy in our partnerships. Between finances, busy schedules, children, and work, few of us create the time to experience a higher plane of being together.

Companionship is truly a source of great joy. My husband and I were walking around the lake recently when he told me how important our companionship is to him. He continued to tell me how much the simple nightly walks we have taken throughout our marriage have provided him with a sense of peace and comfort. You and your partner have committed to walk a lifelong path together. Literally walking together will keep you fit for that commitment.

Sexuality and intimacy are a profound source of joy. The smell of your lover and the touch of his or her skin next to yours can be an intense transporting experience. The pleasure of making love changes over the years of a long marriage. As our bodies begin to sag, droop, and discolor with aging, there is an appreciation of aging together that creates a new dynamic of joy. With each wrinkle and white hair there is spirituality in aging together.

Be mindful of the simple rituals that bring you joy with your partner. Meeting for a cup of coffee, reading to each other, or a simple phone call to say "I love you" during your busy day can sprinkle your life with joy.

Sabbath is a wonderful time to renew joy with your partner. Since the beginning of our marriage we have had a Sabbath devotional time with each other. Each week we read books from a variety of inspirational writers, such as Napoleon Hill, Pema Chodron, Thich Nhat Hanh, or Thomas Merton. Feeding our souls together gives us tremendous intimacy and joy.

I invite you to sit down with a paper and pen with your partner and write down a list of the intimate moments when you each experience joy with each other. Get your calendars out and schedule these into your busy life so you never lose your way.

It's easy for a relationship to stagnate if it is not stirred with passion and care. Know your self first. Then continue to grow in knowledge of each other. Sit together, walk together, talk, and listen to each other's dreams. Take the first step, even if has been a long time since either of you have shown joy. Never stop sharing your hope energy, for it leads to abiding joy.

BEGIN TODAY

What is my excuse for not experiencing joy with my partner?

Ask *Your Self*

Am I focusing on experiencing joy with my partner?

Tell *Your Self*

I am committed to joyful times with my partner.

Give *Your Self*

Take regular walks with your partner.

CHAPTER 32

En-Joy My Family

AWARE OF THE SUFFERING CAUSED BY ANGER, VIOLENCE, AND GRIEF, I AM COMMITTED TO CULTIVATING JOY WITH MY FAMILY.

I felt the powerful consequences of not attending to joy as Brad closed the door to my office. An attractive, wealthy, and powerful man, he entered my office in unimaginable pain. He had come for spiritual direction after the loss of a thirty-five-year marriage, a bout with cancer, and the estrangement of his children.

There just isn't any way to turn back the clock in our lives. Brad grew up poor and was obsessed with becoming wealthy. The focus of his life was growing his business in order to take care of his family and store away lots of money. Brad worked day and night. His business grew to a multimillion-dollar company. His wife would call him to go to his daughter's basketball game. He said he was on the way, but when he looked up at his clock in his office, it was 9 p.m., and he had missed his daughter's game again. His daughter began to despise him, and their relationship became volatile and destructive.

His son became a great baseball player. He vowed not to let his work get in the way of his son's games like it had with his daughter. Brad went to the games, but he stayed on his BlackBerry the entire time, distracted and pacing. He was oblivious to the real reason for his being there.

Brad had become addicted to deals, work, and money. He was always going to change, but before he knew it his daughter and son had graduated from high school. They moved away, and his family life was gone. His wife had unresolved anger, and eventually their marriage fell apart.

I asked Brad what had happened to the joy in his family. He looked down and whispered, "I guess Pamela, my wife, got the joy, and she was always with the kids. I always thought the joy would come later, after we had the money and security and didn't have to worry. But I looked up, and my family was all gone."

In the next year we worked together on how Brad could experience joy in his life. He learned that if you don't have joy yourself, it is impossible to share it with others. Brad experienced a new sense of peace through meditation and in volunteering his service to others.

Months later Brad began visiting with his children and told them he was committed to healing their relationship. It has been a long process of healing, but Brad is a very different person these days. Before he gets out of bed he fills himself with gratitude for the day. His courage has taught me it is never too late to be the wellspring of joy in our world and heal our damaged relationships.

JOY COMES FIRST

The family is in a perilous situation at this moment in history. There is more pressure on the family unit than ever before. Families are bombarded with greater expenses today, not only with higher costs for gasoline, food, clothing, and housing, but also with costs associated with technology and astronomical college expenses for our children.

In addition, we have let technology and the game industry steal our intimate family time and replace it with video games, iPods, teen- and child-oriented TV shows, computer social networking, and endless cell phone conversations that do not promote intimacy.

How does "family joy time" fit into the busy schedules of our children, let alone of the parents? The parents get the family up and ready for the day and head off to their own jobs, only to rush home after work and begin a night at home with chores, balancing kids' homework, keeping up the home, maybe take-home work of their own, and a relationship with a partner. No wonder we all fall into bed each night exhausted.

Parents must take the lead and demonstrate that joy and fulfillment come from peace and balance. You will only have your children under your roof for a short time, so cherish the opportunity to model rituals that promote tending to joy.

Food is a blessing, and mealtimes should be, too. No cell phones or technology allowed at the table. Take thirty minutes of uninterrupted time as a family. Use colorful china, cloth napkins, and say a prayer or observe a moment of silence showing gratitude for your food, the farmers, and the people gathered around the table. Share your day, but keep it light. Meals are not the time for discipline or judgment, but times to enjoy and support one another's presence.

Food preparation can be part of the blessing of mealtime as well, even if there's not time to participate in homemade creations every night. We have always had a garden and canned our food. Eating our homegrown food and preserving it is a great source of joy in our family. The nights our family cans together are nights when memories and stories are created. My daughters and I still laugh at the nights we fell asleep on the couch to the serenade of the lids popping as the canning jars sealed as they cooled.

You must demonstrate balance in your family life. Playing and exercising as a family can be a fountain of joy. Put up a basketball hoop or badminton net in the backyard, and play with your family after dinner each night. Go for evening walks, or bike together in your neighborhood after dinner. When we play we become vulnerable and open our lives to others, and joy flows both ways—in and out.

No matter how stressful the day has been for children or parents, end the day on a positive note. We kept happy music in the family room stereo. For ten minutes every night when our children were young, we would put on fun music, and all four of us would dance around the room laughing and singing. Even now when the adult daughters are home I will grab them in my arms and swing them around the room singing songs from our old-time Disney favorites.

Don't neglect getting away from it all—together. Invite your children to help research where to go on your family vacation. When you plan ahead it creates excitement and anticipation. It doesn't have to be expensive. Set aside an amount of money you can afford to spend, and have everyone explore where you can vacation for that amount of money. You will create lifetime memories of joy for your family. Vacations are also an opportunity for spiritual retreats in nature and for spending more time connecting with the Divine in order to fuel family joy.

Go to the beach and watch the waves together. Swim or wade in the ocean, in rivers, in lakes, streams, and springs. Listen, look, and feel the movement of the natural world.

Every day of your life you are creating everlasting memories for every member of your family. Wake up every morning with the clear intention to create joy in your family. Before you go to sleep at night, review your day with your family and make sure your family had some joy infused with the responsibilities and work. The family who experiences joy together stays together.

BEGIN TODAY

What is my excuse for not creating "joy time" in my family?

Ask *Your Self*

What can I do to begin creating joy in my family today?

Tell *Your Self*

Our family's priority is to experience joy.

Give *Your Self*

Participate in playtime with your children every day.

CHAPTER 33

En-Joy My Work

AWARE OF THE SUFFERING CAUSED BY ANGER, VIOLENCE, AND GRIEF, I AM COMMITTED TO CULTIVATING JOY IN MY WORK.

It was my first real job. I had just turned sixteen, and I was so proud putting on my JCPenney employee badge. I worked in a department that housed four different groups—gift-wrap, layaway, credit, and catalog—with a bunch of older women who were like aunts and mothers to me.

Three of the women were crotchety, but Ms. Jacobs was different. Ms. Jacobs was the "joy queen" at JCPenney. When a disagreeable customer returned a layaway and started raising her voice, Ms. Jacobs would smile, lean forward, and say, "You are right, honey. I agree with you, and I am going to make it right for you. Just wait a little minute." No matter how foul customers got at the counter, she could melt their hearts with pure joy.

Every customer paying on a bill or a layaway would get infected with her joy. "Hey, darling. Oh, what a lovely sweater, and that pin you're wearing looks like it's from Tiffany's." "Is that your beautiful daughter? Well, she looks just like you, angel." Whether it was a nasty employee or a frustrated customer, she would anoint them with her pure joy.

As a young girl my life was changed by this joy mentoring. I learned how not to react to another's emotions but to come from my own center of joy. I couldn't control other people and their emotions and reactions, but I sure could let my joy overflow to them, and most times that changed things.

Ms. Jacobs became my second mother and guided me through some tough times in my life. Some people trust penicillin, Clorox, or disinfectants to get rid of nastiness. Ms. Jacobs said we all just need daily doses of pure joy.

WORK IS CO-CREATION

I am afraid not many people enjoy going to work every day. Work is supposed to be a source of great joy in our lives. I am a Benedictine oblate at a Benedictine monastery. A Benedictine oblate takes a vow to support and live the philosophy of the Benedictine order in the world. Oblates are married or single working people with families who live the Benedictine life out in the world. One of the principles of Benedictine philosophy is that work is holy and a place to experience true joy in one's life. Work is a process of co-creation, and the joy springs from this relationship.

Each of us has a calling in our lives. When you listen to your life and understand what you love, you can experience joy in your work. Joy and work are interwoven.

Work is one of the purposes of our lives. When the Industrial Revolution moved people away from their farms, homes, and families and put them into factories and plants, humans became disconnected from the dignity of their work. Work is to be a source of creativity, productivity, meaning, and joy.

Our DNA knows what we were born to do. When we make choices for money or status or based on our parents' preplanned career choice, we end up with a midlife crisis. We ask the question "What am I doing with my life? Or is this really what it's all about?" The fulfillment of joy from our working doesn't come when work is mechanical but rather when it comes from our heart.

So how can we return to the ancient practice of work being holy and making us whole in the empty, soulless work environment of today?

The concept of work-life balance is based on work returning to some form of balance and joyfulness. Work-life balance policies are becoming a part of many corporations today. We are realizing that meaningless work creates depression and anxiety and can promote physical or mental illness.

With the advent of mind-body medicine we are learning that individuals cannot be chronically stressed or they get sick. Wonderful tools such as flex-time schedules are helping to return joy into the workplace. With technology people can work at the office or from home. Another option is for two people to share the same job so that both have less work pressure, and therefore they can spend more joyful time with their families. This is creating more balance and joy in our lives.

Corporations are looking at the workplace with new eyes and trying to make it a healthier, more meaningful place to be. Architects are designing new workspaces to create more balance and joy in employees' lives. There are programs offered in many corporations to teach staff how to handle stress, anger, and depression. The workplace is changing for the better, thanks to innovative work-life balance programs.

What can you contribute at work to bring comfort and joy? Have a meeting at work in the break room or send an email and ask the staff to list three things they could do at work that would create joy for them. Make a list of all these "joy stations" at work, and meet with your supervisor or manager. Try to integrate some of these joy ideas from the staff into your company's work-life balance program.

Have a covered-dish party once a week at work, or have everyone chip in and get lunch delivered. Take this time to share, laugh, and get to know each other.

Joy at work is discovered when staff are invited to be part of the creative process of the company. Talk to management and discuss ways that the employees can become a part of the creative future of your company.

Meet with your supervisor or boss and set clear goals for your career. Have an agreement with your company that there will be certain rewards when you reach your goals. This creates a feeling of accomplishment and pride in your company and in your life. Make sure each department or division has created specific goals with attached rewards, such as a day off, a company picnic, or some other agreed-upon reward.

We humans live life through our senses. I cannot tell you how many companies I have given speeches to on work-life balance or happiness where their offices look and feel like a colorless, lifeless prison. Creating an enriching work environment sets the stage for experiencing joy at work. Try to incorporate color, photographs, inspirational sayings, music, and light into your workspace.

Work is the process of joyful cocreation. Let's begin to innovate our corporations, companies, factories, and stores with new life, where people can begin to live in joy.

BEGIN TODAY

What is my excuse for not creating joy at work?

Ask *Your Self*

What can I do to create joy at work?

Tell *Your Self*

I am creating joy at work.

Give *Your Self*

Make your workplace a place of joy.

CHAPTER 34

En-Joy My Community

> **AWARE OF THE SUFFERING CAUSED BY ANGER, VIOLENCE, AND GRIEF, I AM COMMITTED TO CULTIVATING JOY IN MY COMMUNITY.**

"If you could just help me get enough money for some haircuts for the kids, that's all I need, Dr. Hall. Our kids just have to experience some joy this week." I was a little confused. What did getting children haircuts have to do with joy? But that was before I knew Mr. Dukes.

Mr. Dukes began working with at-risk middle-school children many years ago. He is the discipline officer for an inner-city school in a very dangerous neighborhood in Atlanta. He was hired to discipline the children who had the most violent behavior. The problem for Mr. Dukes was that he couldn't just discipline each child. Each child had a heart-breaking story, and Mr. Dukes's heart began to bleed.

Soon after he was hired he began taking his own money to buy shoes for the children, or he'd buy groceries for a child's family or pay to have the electricity turned back on for another family. This led him to take a part-time job to help pay for these boys' needs. That is where

I met this angel of joy. He was putting a shoe on my left foot at the store where he worked when out of the blue he asked, "What brings you joy?"

I started laughing. I had never tried on new shoes before and had the salesman ask me what brings me joy. I smiled and said, "I love to help people in lots of different ways. What brings you joy, Mr. Dukes?" (I saw his name on his name tag.) "My kids. My kids bring me joy," he said smiling from ear to ear. "Oh, you have children?" I asked. "Well, I didn't birth any of my own. These are my kids at school."

Two hours later we hugged and decided to join forces to work with these children in need. It has been two years now, and our plans have exceeded all expectations. We have thirty children whom we help clothe, mentor, and educate in self-esteem, manners, and health care.

Mr. Dukes blesses his kids with the balm of joy. He knows they live in horrendously challenging circumstances with broken families, violence, gangs, drugs, and poverty. So he believes his job is to sprinkle their lives with joy. He has created watering holes of joy for the kids. They find joy in simple things like a haircut, a pair of jeans, attending a basketball game, eating pizza, or watching a movie.

It has brought so much joy to my life assisting this joy worker. I am blessed to witness him spreading joy like rainbows that follow the dark clouds. His mantra is "I am blessed to be a blessing." Mr. Dukes calls each of us to look around our communities to see how we can be joy.

COMMUNITY IS LIVING JOY

The neighborhood you live in can be a source of great joy. People love to organize communities around different needs and interests.

There are garden clubs for the lovers of the earth. There are running groups for the people who find joy in running, and mommy groups where young mothers find a source of joy and comfort by sharing time together. Many communities have clubs where they play cards. I belonged to a meditation group where I discovered some of the greatest joy I have ever known.

Your home, work, and faith communities are part of your extended family and can be a source of joy and growth throughout your life.

All religions maintain religious holidays; they create rituals for different life stages and become a place for continuing education and fellowship. When I was Roman Catholic, my life was tightly tied to my religious community. There were the annual religious holidays and then the rituals for the stages of my life. The sacraments are rituals that are tied to every stage of your life. Most of these rituals—baptism, first communion, confirmation, and marriage—are all sources of great joy to be shared in the community of faith. Jews, Muslims, Hindus, and Buddhists all have holy rituals that create and sustain joy in their communities.

Please take the time to explore your passions, and then reach out to find people with common interests. Finding like-minded people to share your passion is pure joy. If there is not a group or community already formed around your interest, start one yourself. Print a flyer and put it into mailboxes to create interest. You will be surprised how your life will transform when you join a community where you share a similar passion. Know that it's our human condition to be in community with one another.

Many of us come out of afflictive families with which we have little or no contact. You can discover a new family in community. There are infinite possibilities for healing and joy in community.

Mr. Dukes's model is an opportunity to heal the wounds of our past family experiences and create new families of our choice in community. Create new stories instead of living old stories. You have tales to tell around the campfire or hearth as the sun sets on the water.

BEGIN TODAY

What is my excuse for not seeking joy in community?

Ask *Your Self*

How can I find like-minded people in my community?

Tell *Your Self*

I am connected to a community that brings me joy.

Give *Your Self*

Commit to time with community on a regular basis.

PART THREE

The Ocean

Human survival is threatened by our greatest peril: our postmodern lifestyle. We have lost reverent respect for ourselves, others, and our natural world. The natural law that governs our universe is the law of cause and effect. We have lived as if there were no consequences for our actions.

The destiny that befalls the ocean is our destiny. The ocean is the foundation of all life on our fragile planet. Our relationship with the ocean is the basis for our human existence. Our human legacy is mirrored in the legacy of the ocean.

Mahatma Gandhi said it perfectly in this poem.

> **In this structure, composed of**
> **innumerable villages,**
> **there will be ever-widening,**
> **never ascending circles.**
> **Life will not be a pyramid**
> **with the apex sustained by the**
> **bottom.**

But it will be an oceanic circle whose centre will be the individual.

Every obstacle is an opportunity: whatever our differences—politics, race, religion, economics, philosophy—we are connected by our Amma, our mother ocean. She has the power to diminish our differences. We are each different rivers flowing into the same ocean. She is the life giver. We cannot survive without her.

Interdependence is the key to sustainability. The blessing of interdependence tells us we are not Chinese, American, African, or Iranian. Our identity is beyond black, white, yellow, or red skin. We are not communist, socialist, or democratic. We are not Jew, Muslim, Christian, Hindu, Buddhist, or atheist. We are human beings created in the image of God who were breathed into existence in this magnificent paradise called Earth. Our life's journey from the river into the ocean is to learn that our survival depends on cooperating with each other and nature.

We are facing our karmic challenge right now in these perilous times. There is a reason, a purpose, we are not all the same race, gender, sexual orientation, national origin, or philosophical bent. There is a reason we all have to move past the illusion of our differences to share our one common destiny determined by our ocean, the air we breathe, the earth that creates our food.

These words attributed to Chief Seattle around 1890 speak succinctly to the charge of the human race as we move forward.

We are part of the earth and it is part of us. The perfumed flowers are our sisters, the deer, the horse, the great eagle,

these are our brothers. The rocky crests, the juices of the meadows, the body heat of pony and man all belong to the same family.

What is a man without beasts? If the beasts were gone, men would die from a great loneliness of spirit. For whatever happens to the beasts soon happens to man. All things are connected.

This we know. The earth does not belong to man, man belongs to the earth.

This we know. All things are connected like the blood which unites one family. All things are connected.

Whatever befalls the earth befalls the sons of the earth. Man did not weave the web of life, he is merely a strand in it. Whatever he does to the web, he does to himself.

The whites, too, shall pass—perhaps sooner than other tribes. Continue to contaminate your own bed, and you might suffocate in your own waste.

*UN*COMMON H.O.P.E. IS THE ANSWER

The Four Commitments of H.O.P.E. can lead us out of the perilous waters into a voyage of *un*common hope. Hope is the healing balm our world cries out for. Not just hope that resides in the hearts of our individual breasts but *un*common hope that knows no borders, boundaries, or limits. We must join each other in an ocean of hope that is vast, deep, and eternal.

Commitment to creating a mindful community begins this moment, in our hearts, minds, and souls. Our mission is to give voice and action to the message of H.O.P.E.—unwavering honesty, optimism, perseverance, and joy.

The same holy blood that courses through our bodies, the same rhythm of our one heart that beats in our chests, and the one Divine sacred breath of life that fills our lungs connects us all.

Separation is an illusion. The ocean eternally teaches us this valuable lesson. All sacred scriptures of all lands and of all peoples echo this truth. Let us join hearts, hands, and voices and commit to our challenging journey.

The Ripple Effect

Everything is energy. Our every minute word and action reverberates into the universe. The repercussions of every single life are immeasurable. Every solitary action of our lives spreads like a ripple in the ocean, affecting untold others.

Each one of us is a pebble of hope. As we drop our pebble of hope into the ocean, the ripple effect of our lives can heal our planet and one another.

I challenge you to go into the world and live an extraordinary life of H.O.P.E. Our pebbles uniting can create the ripple effect we need to create *un*common H.O.P.E. to save our world.

Amma Kathleen

Epilogue

On the day I finished this book, I went to the stable to check on our pregnant mare, Karma, who was due to foal in two weeks. As I slid the stall door open, there on the shavings was her newborn foal, who had arrived early. We named her Uncommon Hope.

About the Author

Dr. Kathleen Hall, internationally recognized lifestyle expert in stress and work-life balance, is the founder and CEO of The Stress Institute (stressinstitute.com), The Mindful Living Network (mindfullivingtv.com), and Alter Your Life (alteryourlife.com). Her advice has been featured by all the major national media, including NBC's *Today* show, *Anderson Cooper 360*, Oprah and Friends, Martha Stewart Radio, *Working Woman*, *Woman's Day*, and *Parade*.

Dr. Hall earned a bachelor of science in finance from Jacksonville State University, a master of divinity from Emory University, and a doctorate in spirituality from Columbia Theological Seminary. Her diverse background of study with medical pioneers includes Dr. Dean Ornish of the Preventive Medicine Research Institute, Dr. Herbert Benson at the Harvard Mind/Body Institute, Dr. Jon Kabat-Zinn at the University of Massachusetts Stress Reduction Clinic, as well as the Dalai Lama, Thich Nhat Hanh, Desmond Tutu, Jimmy Carter, and others. Dr. Hall has perfected her expertise in these related fields—"Where Science Meets the Soul."

She is also the global ambassador for the Unilever/Knorr Soup campaign Eat Soup, Live Healthy; world thought leader to Fortune 500 corporations; Electronic Arts spokesperson (pogo.com); Darden Restaurant spokesperson; Tempur-Pedic spokesperson; Princess Cruise Line spokesperson, Microsoft spokesperson, and stress and work-life balance expert for ClubMom.com, w2w, and Momcorps.com. In fact, Martha Stewart Publications named her the "Stress Queen."

Dr. Hall lives on her horse farm, Oak Haven, with her family, where she maintains a bird sanctuary and rescues animals outside of Atlanta, Georgia.